THE SECOND COMING
of CHRIST

Rudolf Joseph Lorenz Steiner
February 27, 1861 – March 30, 1925

FROM THE WORKS OF DR. RUDOLF STEINER

THE SECOND COMING of CHRIST

IN THE ETHERIC REALM

Dr. Douglas J. Gabriel

Our Spirit, LLC
2024

OUR SPIRIT, LLC

P. O. Box 355

Northville, MI 48167
www.ourspirit.com
www.neoanthroposophy.com
www.gospelofsophia.com
www.eternalcurriculum.com

2023 Copyright © by Our Spirit, LLC

All rights reserved. No part of this publication may
Be reproduced, stored in a retrieval system, or transmitted,
in any form or by any means, electronic, mechanical,
recording, photocopying, or otherwise, without prior written
permission of the publisher.

ISBN: 978-1-963709-99-5

Book Cover art by Charles Andrade at www.lazure.com

CONTENTS

What is the Etheric Second Coming of Christ?   1
    Rudolf Steiner's Indications   31
The Damascus Event as the Second Coming   35
    Rudolf Steiner on the Damascus Event   40
The Biography of the Great I Am   65
    Harvest Gods and Solar Heroes   70
    Christ has Always Been Present   72
    Adam Kadmon   74
    Christ's Influence on Human Development   80
The 'I Am' and Thou through Education   91
The Nature of Christ—the 'I Am'   101
    The Great 'I Am' Throughout History   106
    Ancient India   107
    Ancient Persia   111
    Egypt/Chaldea/Sumeria   112
    Norse Mythology   114
    Celtic   116
    Finnish Kalevala   116
    Hebrew   117
    Greek   117

Roman	119
Americas	120
Rudolf Steiner on the Pre-Earthly Deeds of Christ	123
Krishna—Christ's Pre-Earthly Deed in India	154
Incarnations of Lord Vishnu (Krishna) the Sustainer	165
Perfected Copies of Christ's Bodies	167
Conclusion	183
Michaelic Verse by Rudolf Steiner	185
Bibliography	187
Diagrams	193
About Dr. Rudolf Steiner	197
About the Author, Dr. Douglas Gabriel	199
Translator's Note	201

What is the Etheric Second Coming of Christ?

Rudolf Steiner gave the world the most comprehensive picture of the nature of Christ, which is called the "Wisdom (Sophia) of the Cosmic Christ," which can be found in any mythology, religion, philosophy, or theosophical cosmology. His sweeping insights arise from his natural clairvoyance tempered by a philosophical and scientific approach to a living cosmology of spiritual hierarchies who manifest the created world that our senses behold. Steiner's lectures entitled, *The Fifth Gospel* talk about the esoteric secrets of the missing years of the life of Jesus of Nazareth and about Mary Sophia (called the Mother of Jesus) and the hidden mysteries of the *Gospels*. Volume I of *The Gospel of Sophia,* by Tyla Gabriel was inspired by Steiner's insights concerning the *Bible* and the descriptions of the life of Christ found in the *Fifth Gospel*. The secrets concerning the 'two Jesus children,' the 'two Marys' and the 'two Johns,' are profoundly inspired Wisdom-teachings that lift the veil hiding the true nature of the Cosmic Christ. These Christian mysteries have been guarded for centuries by Freemasonic and Rosicrucian Orders but are revealed in our time because the veil between the seen and unseen has been drawn aside.

The Mysteries of the Etheric Christ, the Second Coming of Christ in the Etheric Realm, are derived from a number of lecture cycles Rudolf Steiner gave on the topic. Steiner's revelations on the Second Coming of Christ have been corroborated by many modern clairvoyants who can see Christ's Second Coming in the Etheric Realm through direct clairvoyant perception. All that Dr. Steiner taught about this 'second greatest event in human evolution' has been found to be accurate and is applicable to our modern circumstances. An initiate can see through the astral light into the etheric realm and see that Christ's resurrected etheric body has fully surrounded the etheric body of the Earth and is bringing back to life that which was dying through entropy. Christ's deed of re-enlivening the life-body of the Earth, and the human life-body, was necessary to turn death into life, entropy into ectropy so that human spiritual development could continue to evolve. Christ's newest 'deed' of resurrecting the etheric life of the Earth and the human etheric body is the fifth deed that Christ has already accomplished to create, sustain, and re-enliven human physical, soul, and spiritual development. These are the mysteries of the Wisdom of the Cosmic Christ, the Sophia of Christ, that Steiner spoke about so often. We will hear about these numerous Pre-Earthly, Earthly, and Future Deeds of Christ throughout this book, once a foundation is presented that can aid in beholding the Cosmic 'I Am' and His biography that is so inextricably intertwined with the 'I Am' of the human being.

It is the Wisdom/Sophia of the Cosmic Christ that the Maitreya Buddha [current Bodhisattva] teaches in our time and will continue to teach into the future as his main message for the ascent of humanity. It may seem strange that Buddhas and Bodhisattvas are concerned with the current Deeds of Christ. That is because Christ is beyond any religion, He is a living, active Being who is known by all other spiritual beings, no matter their names or religious affiliations. The secrets of the Etheric Christ will also be revealed by the great Kalki Avatar because both the Maitreya Buddha and the Kalki Avatar work directly for Christ and Sophia in the spiritual world in the Mother Lodge of Humanity. The past and the future meet when these two streams unite as Sophia Christos—the Wisdom of the Cosmic Christ. An accurate understanding of what Christ and Sophia have already accomplished in the past is necessary to comprehend what Steiner called the Turning Point of Time, or the Mystery of Golgotha; for Christ died on the Mount of Calvary called Golgotha.

Christ's incarnation into the body of Jesus of Nazareth lasted for three and a half years only. There will not be another incarnation of Christ in a physical body. Christ Jesus conquered the physical realm and redeemed the over-hardened material world by the selfless sacrifice of a God humbly enduring a human death and the subsequent descent into hell and resurrection from the dead. Christ Jesus went to the core of the Earth and built a golden altar upon which Christ-like actions are offered to the heavens by all those who come after Him and also conquer death. Christ redeemed the Earth through his resurrection and by conquering death. Christ is now helping humanity turn the 'Planet Earth' into a radiant 'Sun Earth.' Through the auroral polar lights, new light is born from human spiritual deeds as a beginning to the Earth shining outwardly and transforming into a future Sun or Star. Christ's deed was the turning point for the Earth, and humanity—from darkness to light. That is why Dr. Steiner calls this fourth deed of Christ, the Turning Point of Time.

Christ will not come again in a physical body because He no longer needs to descend that far down the ranks of the spiritual hierarchies after accomplishing His cosmic redemption of the Earth and humanity. At this point in time, Christ comes down into the realm of the Angels and Archangels, the etheric realms. Christ has risen to heaven but appears wherever 'two or more are gathered in His name,' in the development of their Christened souls. Christ must now redeem the dying etheric realm of the Earth and the human etheric body. The etheric body is essentially an 'eternal youth' who builds up the physical body through forces of alternating levity and gravity working through the ethers and the etheric formative forces. The etheric body of the Earth encompasses the elements of earth, water, air, fire, light, sound, and life. These elements and ethers are manipulated by science into electrical and electromagnetic forces as a 'shadow substance' of spirit that draws life out of humans, instead of building up the life forces that Christ brings.

We can see that humanity has spoiled the earth, water, air, and warmth of our planet. We have also poisoned our human body's elements and ethers and used the stomach, blood stream, and the senses as a dumping ground for toxic waste. Humans have defiled the Earth and the human body with evil machinations that attempt to kill the soul and spirit. The result becomes the inability to connect with the 'Earthly and Cosmic Nutrition Stream,' thereby starving the spiritual world and our own body, soul, and spirit. The etheric realms of the Earth and the human body are in dramatic 'end of times' apocalypse fever. The apocalypse of *Revelation* is happening now, in our environment and in our bodies. The dragon of materialism has taken the human body hostage and is demanding that our thoughts, feelings, and deeds be given over to the Dragon, the Beast, and Satan. Christ is battling for 'pure souls' against the Dragon of ten heads, the two-horned Beast, and Satan, and is trying to keep the etheric realm alive and healthy during the incessant onslaught. Truly, Christ is being crucified again by the dark war of materialism against human beings. There is a battle raging against humanity's spiritual destiny and only the Second Coming of Christ can win the victory.

True spiritual Moral Imaginations, Moral Inspirations, and Moral Intuitions feed the spiritual world and thus the spiritual world returns in kind with heavenly dew, the elixir of life, ambrosia and nectar, and the philosopher's stone as reciprocal nourishment. The etheric world dies when dead, cold, brain-bound thinking makes lifeless gray shadow thoughts with materialistic concepts. Human spiritual thought builds up the ethers while gray shadow thoughts kill the ethers and don't allow for new spiritual matter to be created in the human heart. This would be similar to all plants on the Earth dying and thereby ending the production of oxygen. Subsequently, humans would die without the oxygen created by plants. Likewise, the spiritual world and our bodies are in a symbiotic relationship of nourishment. We are not the highest organism on the food chain. We create food for the gods, and they create the spiritual nourishment our souls need to be able to fuel the search for spirit, for wisdom and love.

There is an etheric realm around the Earth that interpenetrates all life on the planet. This etheric realm is the womb of life on Earth. It is the body of the Mother of All, Sophia the Goddess of Wisdom. She is being killed by technologies that humans have not evolved high enough to utilize with wisdom. We are on a dying planet that some materialists want to kill even quicker. The thoughtless ones want immediate personal gain and gratification, and then they will leave the Earth behind as a trash can. This is offset by Christ's deed in the realm of the living etheric formative forces. He has come to re-enliven the etheric realm and make it new, just as He has already done with the physical Earth. Christ will resurrect the etheric realm and save the sources of life that renew the physical realm.

Rudolf Steiner pointed out that the Mystery of Golgotha was the 'greatest event in world history.' He also said that the Mystery of Christ's resurrection in the etheric realm of the Earth is the 'second most important event in history.' Essentially, history could end if Christ is not successful. Christ needs every person, who knows eternal life in their heart, to help enthrone Christ's nature in their thinking, feeling and willpower ("Not I but Christ in me"). Moral Imaginations need to enkindle spiritual deeds so that the etheric realm can be filled with the warmth of spiritual thoughts imbued with the light of wisdom. Each person who develops a living cosmology of Christ, that places Him as the cosmic and human solution to the challenges of the forces of death, can be a gardener who plants the seeds of the Tree of Life in their heart that all may live in love and happiness. We can be sky-walkers and heroines of the Labors of Sophia who re-enliven a new Moral Imagination of the Wisdom of Christ, Sophia Christos. These Moral Imaginations of Wisdom's Love of Christ can feed our souls and renew the Earth,-- 'and I saw a new heaven and a new Earth.'

Rudolf Steiner indicated in his book, *The Reappearance of the Christ in the Etheric*, that Christ would start to appear to some people around 1933, and beyond, in a 'new type of spiritual vision.' He also said that many people would start to experience the Etheric Christ in the fashion that Paul experienced Christ on the road to Damascus. One could say that this Damascus Event is similar to witnessing the ascension body that Christ developed before He died. This ascension body is a body created out of etheric substance instead of physical substance. Christ can utilize the entire etheric body of the Earth to congeal His form wherever and whenever He wishes. This manifestation is in advance of what all people will be able to experience in the far future. At that time, Sophia and Christ will walk among us and be with us whenever we need them.

It has often been imagined that Christ will appear to the whole world in a rapture moment, 'seen from East to West, coming on a cloud.' This vision of the Second Coming of Christ is confused with the apocalyptic accounts of Christ manifesting as the 'judge of time.' The moment of death, sleep, or when the aspirant consciously crosses of the threshold to the spiritual world are opportunities for a personal apocalypse to appear. The aspirant will experience Christ during that revelation, because Christ is the Guardian of the Threshold. Christ, no longer the Egyptian God Anubis, weighs and judges the soul to see if it has gained spiritual merit. Christ stands at the threshold between the physical and spiritual worlds as the Lord of Karma, the one who weighs the merit of the soul. Truly, death is an awful apocalypse for the materialistic person who has been killing the etheric realm and not receiving spiritual nourishment. Materialistic beliefs create a terrifying experience of fear, doubt, and hatred as the unredeemed aspects of the soul that cannot cross into the spiritual realm burn the soul clean in a fiery hell-realm of sorts. As Christ is working hard to enliven the etheric realms, the materialistic thinker is killing their soul and starving the spiritual world.

The battle for the life of the etheric is another 'war in heaven.' Lucifer and Ahriman, pride and fear, have been loosed upon the Earth and are trying to steal the wings of every human soul so they cannot rise-up to the etheric realm and find nourishment. These evil specters, Lucifer and Ahriman, can be tamed and properly utilized by the Christ forces in the human soul. Balancing the trinity of thinking, feeling, and willing is a prerequisite for conquering the evil forces that would like to steal life-force (etheric force) from humans.

There is a wonderful source of ever-renewing forces of life surrounding the Earth. It is called the super-etheric realm of the Earth, or Shambhala (also: Shamballa) in the East, and New Jerusalem or Eden Redeemed in the West. This realm has been claimed by Sophia Christos as the redeemed part of the etheric already under their control. Every perfected body of a saint, avatar, bodhisattva, or spiritual person is imprinted and saved for all time to come in this etheric realm. Once a perfected 'vehicle' is imprinted into this realm, it is available to copy itself for the use of other initiates who wish to embody it and are pure and selfless enough to hold this perfection. This super-etheric realm is also called by Rudolf Steiner the 'Realm of Spiritual Economy' where Spirit employs wise economy by replicating perfected bodies for those in like resonance.

One of the most profound secrets concerning the Realm of Spiritual Economy is that the perfected bodies of Christ Jesus and Mary Sophia are imprinted in the super-etheric realm of Shambhala. St. Augustine, Johannes Tauler, Meister Eckhart, St. Francis, and Rudolf Steiner all used one or more perfected vehicles from this realm. There is no need to create other perfected vehicles, because the spirit knows how to utilize something like multi-dimensional holographic mirroring in the processes of creation and maintenance of the Universe—the microcosm is the image of the macrocosm. Humans who are emulating Christ, Sophia, saints, and great thinkers may use this realm of spiritual economy and embody the wisdom available in many ways.

Christ joined His physical karma with the Earth as a whole and gave His life to re-enkindle the forces of life that were waning. The Earth, as a whole, would have died and humanity would have failed in its evolution to become Angels without Christ's intervention. Christ's blood and body went into the Earth and His spirit descended to its core. When Christ rose from the dead, He brought the new etheric physical life of the Earth along with Him. After ascending to heaven, Christ is now actively bringing the dying etheric realm of the Earth, and the human etheric body, along with Him again in His continuing ascent from the physical, to the etheric and to the astral and Ego ('I Am') realms in the future. The battle is engaged, but the victory is not won yet. Each human soul is an entire world and a separate battleground inside himself. Worlds are being lost to Lucifer, Ahriman, and Sorat inspired Asuric beings who wish to bind thinking to sense-bound desire of the physical and not let Christ enliven their thoughts with spiritual, Moral Imaginations. Christ is offering wisdom, love, and the 'waters of life' in the realms of the super-etheric; whereas, demons offer lies, jealousy, and evil that drains life from the etheric body.

Materialistic enslavement to physical pleasures and hedonistic selfishness darkens the spiritual world at night when sense-bound thinker's sleep. Instead of shining like a star as they sleep, the materialist weaves spider webs of desire that are colorless and filled with grotesque desires that bind the soul to earthly matter. Their nights are filled with horrors and fears instead of the light and nourishment from the spiritual food of the gods. They fight demons all night who are 'living darkness' that swallows light. They remain bound to the Earth and the fiery hells that arise from desire and addictions to the Seven Deadly Sins.

Reading spiritual content and thinking about it is a banquet for the gods. Reflecting and meditating on spiritual substance is a fountain of living water that refreshes and nourishes your Guardian Angel. Prayer and spiritual practices are solemn rituals of communion with the spirit, dialogues that nurture both sides. A good conversation about lofty ideas will raise the human spirit, so too, it feeds the spiritual world. As a wondrous spirit-filled dream continues to impress living pictures and Moral Imaginations upon the soul for long periods of time, so too, the loving deeds of a human light up the etheric world and drive away the darkness. By seeking initiation and having the desire to embody the spirit, the aspirant joins in the battle for the etheric realm with every spiritual thought, feeling, or deed.

Christ continues His ascent through the physical, etheric, astral, and Ego realms. Each new realm needs a 'new turning point in time' to align it with the macrocosmic evolution of Christ as He brings the Earth and humanity along with His development. Christ redeemed the physical and is now trying to permanently redeem the etheric realm. We are the battleground; sides have been chosen and you are on a team whether you know it or not. Self-initiation is to 'know yourself, so that you might know the gods and the world.' It is taking responsibility for your own development and being a witness and participant in the new War in Heaven, the battle for the etheric realm and the Appearance of the Second Coming of Christ in the Etheric Realm.

Ahriman is the being of fear that drives humans to lie and sin for the sake of selfish pursuits justified by jealousy and hatred. He wants humans to have cold hearts that believe in nothing but selfishness. He brings death and destruction with him and revels in destroying human spiritual effort. He loves to clip the wings of spirit and bind humans to a mountain where a vulture eats his liver each day. Ahriman is darkness in the realm of thinking. He extinguishes radiant light in favor of cold gray light that mesmerizes but does need feed the soul. He is the father of lies and knows nothing of Christ and His love.

Ahriman is the dragon of materialism, and he is depicted in *Revelations* as ready to consume the 'child of spirit' that is about to be birthed by the 'Woman Clothed with the Sun.' She is our soul, and the child is our spirit. Ahriman would like to make Christ seem like a false dream or a hope of the weak-minded. Ahriman can convince anyone, with endless data, that Christ doesn't exist. Ahriman and

Lucifer cannot see Christ at all for they are both blind to the 'middle realm' of Christ because they work in extremes. All three forces of evil that wish to consume the physical, etheric, and astral and ego bodies of human beings, are active in our time. Many people are blind to this battle and do not know that their soul is being fought over. In the West, Ahriman is winning the battle of deadening the soul and binding it to materialism. The battle is waging, and demonic weapons are being used all around us in an attempt to permanently darken the etheric realm and dampen the fires of Moral Imagination.

Seeing Christ in the etheric realm is a cure for the illness of materialism. Christ engenders love, and love creates light that reveals the wisdom of the divine. Christ implanted a drop of His blood that was enlivened through the Mystery of Golgotha into every human heart. This etheric drop brings the 'light of life' that illuminates the way back to heaven and feeds our soul and spiritual hunger. In the darkest times, this light will draw Christ to us if we are in desperate need of His presence. Often, at the lowest point in a person's life, Christ will walk into the room and heal them. This has been reported many times by people who have intended to commit suicide, but didn't, after Christ appeared to them. Steiner pointed out that after 1933 Christ would appear more and more to people and that if they report it, those who witnessed this wondrous event might be locked up in a psych ward and considered crazy.

At the same time, those aspirants who have advanced along the path will also be able to develop 'etheric vision' that will be able to see Christ and His manifestations in the etheric realm. This new 'etheric vision' will be able to witness Christ active in a variety of ways in the resurrected etheric formative forces. The Etheric Christ will be visible to advanced souls and His presence can be with them on a continuous basis. Christ manifests in the etheric realm and is visible for those with 'eyes to see.'

One Moral Imagination of Christ in the etheric realm is found in the aurora borealis. Just as in the human etherization of the blood, the

Earth, as a whole, etherizes elements that are fueled by forces of human spiritual activity that rise-up from the core of the Earth towards the magnetic north (and south) pole flowing along the magnetic lines of the Van Allen belts. When solar wind collides with these rising ionized elemental particles, a fantastic light display illuminates the sky. This 'new light' from the Earth creates the first self-generated 'starlight' of our new Earth-Sun. One could say that the Christened efforts of humanity light up the Earth with a halo. This also happens in the human body and appears to a clairvoyant as a 'rainbow light' emitted from the midbrain that lights up the aura making it shine like a halo. Saints are noted for creating this 'rainbow bridge' and halo naturally. The human etheric body and the Earth's etheric body have many similar correspondences.

The aurora borealis is a living Imagination of what happens in the human body through the wise and loving interactions between Sophia (soul) and Christ (spirit). When the baptism of fire (Pentecost) alights upon the brow of the initiate, we can see the forces of Christ illuminating the Christened self of the individual. Christ heals the etheric body of the Earth and the etheric body of the individual through a new World Pentecost.

Rudolf Steiner indicated in, *The Reappearance of Christ in the Etheric*, Lecture I: *The Event of the Appearance of Christ in the Etheric World*, that: "the Etheric Christ would be able to be seen especially in 1933, 1935, and 1937." Clairvoyant capacities will become 'natural abilities.' Great changes will take place, and 'Biblical prophecies will be fulfilled.' Human souls will begin to develop 'new faculties out of themselves', to exhibit 'clairvoyant powers.' He said that: "a new age is at hand, in which the souls of human beings must take a step upward into the kingdom of heaven." Then, Christ will reappear because human beings will be raising themselves toward Him in 'etheric vision.' Spiritual Science is preparation for the return of Christ. Just as Paul, others will be "convinced through experiences in the etheric realm that Christ truly lives." Steiner said that the "greatest mystery of our time is the second coming of Christ." Human beings must advance to this 'etheric vision' and see it within their own etheric body. Steiner speaks of the 'Second Coming of Christ' and tells us that we must "raise ourselves up to Christ in the spiritual world by acquiring etheric vision." If humanity were to ignore the Second Coming of Christ in the Etheric, the "vision of Christ in the etheric body would be limited to those who, through esoteric training, prove themselves to be ready to rise to such an experience."

In Lecture II: *The Reappearance of Christ in the Etheric—Spiritual Science as Preparation for a New Etheric Vision*, Steiner indicates that Paul was convinced Jesus was Christ when he "saw Christ clairvoyantly in the atmosphere of the Earth." Paul became convinced that the descent of Christ to the earth consummated the ancient mysteries. Paul's experience of Christ in the 'atmosphere of the earth' can be clairvoyantly experienced after 'esoteric schooling' or through 'natural clairvoyance' that will become 'entirely natural to humanity.' This 'Damascus Event' will be experienced by many people after 1933 as a 'return of Christ.' Christ is present for all those who are able to ascend as far as the 'vision of the etheric body.' He is always present within the 'etheric atmosphere of the earth.' The Second Coming of Christ will happen when human beings advance to 'beholding Christ in the etheric.'

In Lecture V: *The Reappearance of Christ in the Etheric*, Dr. Steiner indicates that initiates in the past always went to 'an ancient country' in order to 'fetch from it' the guiding impulses of humanity and the 'strength and wisdom for their missions.' This land is often referred to as Shambhala or the fountainhead of the super-etheric realm, and ancient clairvoyants could see into these worlds like some sort of fairyland. This land of Shambhala is said to have risen-up into the atmosphere and became invisible. Shambhala will be seen again, at first only for a few, then for more and more human beings. This light-woven, light-gleaming Shambhala abounds in infinite fullness of life that fills hearts with wisdom. Christ is the Lord of this realm.

It is from this realm that the understanding of the cosmic nature of the deed of Christ flows forth as wisdom. The more humans can witness Christ in this realm, the more they will be able to understand the Wisdom in the *Gospels*. As we grow into this mysterious land of Shambhala, it is possible to have a Damascus Event wherein the aspirant directly encounters the living Christ in the etheric realm, just as Paul did on the road to Damascus. The initiate rises into this land and can directly have the Damascus Event as part of self-initiation, a kind of etheric revelation or apocalypse, an 'uncovering of the soul.' This experience can be the foundation for a 'new faith' or 'religion of one.' A direct dialogue begins with the being of Christ as He appears there as a 'second coming' for the awakened initiate.

Christ only comes to Earth once in a physical body and now appears in His etheric body to awakened souls as a 'natural initiation.' According to the level of an initiate, a spiritual kingdom can be felt arising around him as he is led by Christ. Christ will be acknowledged by all who rise into the etheric realm, no matter what prior religious affiliations. Clear waking consciousness is the tool needed to enter this land under the guidance of Christ. The initiate must go there often to draw new forces from the radiant wisdom-filled light and cross the bridge to the land of the super-etheric, Shambhala.

Dr. Steiner goes further to say that new faculties will arise in humanity that will be able to perceive the human etheric body. Another capacity will develop wherein the aspirant will be able to look within himself and behold a dream-like picture that is the karmic outcome of a deed about to be performed. This is a prefiguring or precognitive perception but not a dream. It is 'seeing into the karma of a deed,' a sort of taking responsibility for the karmic outcome of an action.

There will also be the experience of Christ that Paul had before Damascus, but now instead of it being a personal experience, it will become a common experience for certain people. Paul could only be convinced that Jesus was the Christ through a direct clairvoyant experience of Christ in the etheric realm. This clairvoyant experience will be more and more common in the future. Many people will have a direct encounter with the living being of Christ in the etheric realm as a 'second coming.' Previously, only initiates could reach this realm through initiation. All of the faculties attained by initiation will become universal faculties of humanity in the future. Human beings with etheric clairvoyance will behold the Christ appearing before them in an etheric body. This etheric vision is a spiritual seed in the soul that awaits development by the individual. This development is in the hands of the individual.

Etheric clairvoyance can appear without individuals understanding its meaning and can be interpreted as delusion, fantasy, and mental illness. We must be ready to help and understand those who may appear to be psychologically ill, but in fact are witnessing the etheric sphere. People should have this experience in a healthy way as part of spiritual development. It is imperative that Christ be found in the etheric realm before death because the individual cannot come to an understanding of Christ's physical incarnation after death. This is a most important spiritual task, to encounter Christ in the etheric while alive on the Earth so that the Wisdom (Sophia) of Christ can accompany the aspirant through death. It is the development of the higher senses and sense organs that allow this vision of the Etheric Christ to arise.

As we can surmise from hearing Dr. Steiner's profound insight concerning the Etheric Christ, he is the prophet of this 'second greatest event in human spiritual history.' Steiner gave us a prophecy that has already come to pass. There are many accounts since 1933 of Christ manifesting to people who were in great despair. Just as Steiner predicted, some of these people were deemed crazy and locked away. Often, the encounters left people believing they had met Jesus or that they were Jesus. This delusion did not stop with supposedly insane people but many, many people claim to be Jesus reincarnated. The list is long, and the stories are familiar. Many teachers claim to be Christ or Mary Magdalene or Jesus and Mary together in one body, and so on.

Through the work of Rudolf Steiner, we have deep insights into the Etheric Christ and His Second Coming. The Mystery of Golgotha was preceded by three supersensible Pre-Earthly Deeds on the part of Christ. The first event had to do with the harmonizing of the twelve (12) senses in the physical body; the second with the healing of the seven (7) life-processes in man's etheric body; and finally, the third cosmic deed of Christ led to the three (3) fundamental forces of the human soul—thinking, feeling and will—being brought into the necessary equilibrium for a right development of the Ego ('I am').

Christ, once He descended to the Earth, resurrected, and is ascending beyond the physical condition of an earthly human being into an etheric being—the Etheric Christ. Later, Christ will continue to ascend through the astral realm and the realm of the Ego. Eventually, Christ will become the Spirit of the Earth and the Group Soul of Christened human beings. Christ rises to higher stages bringing humanity along. Christ's appearance in the etheric realm was already perceptible for an initiate from 1909 onwards through the astral light. The Etheric Christ became accessible to humanity as a whole through supersensible perception from the 1930s onwards.

Anthroposophy is a new language with which an individual can have a dialogue with Christ. It is the language of the Etheric Christ, the language of spiritual science. Anthroposophy is the language of the spirit with which the Etheric Christ can be understood. Your Spiritual Soul can be born from the understanding of the cosmic nature of Christ provided by Rudolf Steiner's Christian cosmology.

The being of Anthroposophia (Sophia) can be experienced supersensibly through thinking that has risen to apprehend the world of Moral Imaginations. Moral Imaginations received their form through the love that was given by Christ to humanity. What is revealed through Moral Intuition can be attained only by developing and spiritualizing to the highest degree the capacity for love. A person must be able to make this capacity for love into a cognitional force through understanding the Wisdom of the Cosmic Christ which is provided by Sophia and the Spirits of Wisdom—the Kyriotetes.

The Etheric Christ Himself will someday be spiritually embodied in the being Anthroposophia, in order to be received together with Her into the human Ego. When one lets Anthroposophia directly into one's heart, She approaches our soul, knocks 'at the portal of our heart…and says: Let me in, for I am you yourself, I am your true human nature.' Then, Anthroposophia will be the new Grail chalice in the spiritual world receiving Christ within Herself and joining forces with human beings. The nature of that holy chalice is the mystery of Christ's Ego, the eternal Ego which every human Ego can become part of. Copies of Christ's Ego are preserved in the Holy Grail vessel, which is there for those who collaborate with Christ in the realm of Shambhala.

The development of the Christ Ego entails transformation of thinking in the head, to hearing the spiritual word through the supersensible organ of the larynx, and finally to the freeing of the heart from the powers of the Dragon through the Archangel [Archi] Michael's impulses. Through the process of thinking developing into Moral Imagination, the aspirant can perceive Christ in the etheric realm. Through higher speaking (feeling), Moral Inspiration can bring answers to questions posed in the Language of the Spirit directly from Christ to the worthy aspirant. Through the forces of uprightness, Moral Intuition can bring experiences of Christ as the Lord of Karma into the destiny of the aspirant.

It is the task of the aspirant to lift the veil of the New Isis and to rise-up to conscious clairvoyance that can witness the Etheric Christ. This allows the aspirant to attain the golden halo of genuine wisdom—the Sophia of Christ. This step of self-development brings a new sacramentalism and communion with Christ as the World Ego through the sounding Word (Logos) and through moral deeds. There will be ever-new revelations of Christ in the future. To witness and understand these revelations requires the aspirant to merge the two streams of etherized blood (front and back spinal columns) and attain perception of the Etheric Christ. When the Tree of Knowledge and the Tree of Life intertwine and rise out of the heart towards the head, this creates the new Tree of Paradise. Through this process, Christ transforms human memory and conscience into supersensible organs that can perceive the workings of spirit.

Adam is connected to the Tree of Knowledge, whereas Adam Kadmon is connected to the Tree of Life and is the guardian and preserver of man's eternal image, as created by the gods. The new Tree of Paradise is the World-Tree of the Etheric Christ who has redeemed Eden through His sacrifices and reclaimed Paradise. This Tree of Paradise brings the new life needed to save the etheric realms of the earth and the human body.

To develop the supersensible organs to perceive Christ's Second Coming in the realm of Shamballa, the aspirant should train the astral body to become a sheath for the astral body of Christ to use. This sheath is developed through wonder, astonishment, devotion, and reverence towards the spirit. To develop the etheric sheath for Christ to utilize, the aspirant should express love and compassion towards all beings and must purify his conscience into a new transformative consciousness that contributes to the work of the Group Ego of Christened Humanity. This development leads the aspirant to understand Christ's role as the Lord of Karma. These etheric sheaths as receptacles (grails) for Christ are developed through wonder, wisdom, love, and conscience.

Many claims of being Christ are simply misunderstandings that arise in the second stage of initiation called the 'completion stage.' In this stage of spiritual practice, the object of worship literally becomes the aspirant who is worshipping the deity. The aspirant becomes identified with the deity they are worshiping. Thus, people have an encounter with Christ in the etheric and then they believe they are Christ. It is true that the higher self of the aspirant and Christ are intertwined. To see your higher self, is to see Christ. But then to extrapolate that you are Christ, is simple confusion that arises through the mirror images created in the astral light during the first stage of spiritual development. If the aspirant's astral body is not purified, problems arise when he enters the spiritual world. The aspirant may encounter Christ and think that they are the being they behold. Thus, many people claim to be Christ after experiencing Him in the etheric realm. A few decades ago, this served as proof that a person was insane and should be locked up and given drugs to end the delusion.

Now-a-days, when someone says they are the reincarnation of Jesus Christ, no one bats an eye. Many new age teachers believe they are Christ reincarnated, and when that isn't impressive enough, they claim to be the Maitreya Buddha, the Kalki Avatar, or Sophia Herself. This type of immature identification with the human astral body's tendency to create mirror images is quite common. Some teachers have developed stigmata or do not eat food as further confirmation of their spiritual authenticity. We should all work through the passion of Christ and the deeds of great spiritual teachers to find the best models to follow. Living Christ's life as an 'imitation' would also now include Christ's further development through the resurrection of the etheric realm. Christ is resurrected and alive in the etheric realm, not physically crucified over and over again. The mysteries of Easter and resurrection should accompany any healthy image of Christ and therefore stigmata and inedia are no longer appropriate stages of initiation to linger in.

To reach the etheric body, the aspirant must first advance through the more immediate concern of the astral body. The astral body of desires impresses its good and bad habits on the time-body of the etheric. Before you can reach Christ in the etheric, you usually must tame the astral body of desires. The aspirant will not methodically advance without stopping bad habits and developing new spiritual habits that impress healthy rhythms into the etheric body. Daily prayer, meditation, and spiritual practice must be well established before the aspirant can successfully look into the realm of Shambhala. The aspirant must stop the habits that create astral impurities and then the positive spiritual habits can help raise the aspirant to the astral light and then etheric vision.

References to rising and going up into the etheric realm refer to the super-etheric sphere around the Earth. There is also the etheric body of the human being. The two etheric bodies are connected but different. We rise-up to the super-etheric, but we look inside our own bodies to find the personal, human etheric body. The forces of warmth and light alternate with sound and life in both etheric realms. In the near future, we will be able to look into the super-etheric sphere with the help of the human etheric body and find the connecting links. When a human beholds the etheric body with etheric vision, Christ is seen in the human etheric body and the super-etheric sphere. The same mechanisms underlie the development of new spiritual organs that are commonly used by initiates and will become more and more available for humanity over the next two thousand years. Initiates are the avant-garde of human development.

If an aspirant wishes to become an initiate, the path lies through the astral body into the etheric body and ultimately into the physical body. The astral body is the battleground of emotions and suffering; Christ works to calm and bring peace to this realm. Christ can simply "take on" an etheric form and manifest before a suffering person and bring comfort. Many people, in great moments of despair, have experienced this type of visitation. These people may not have been initiates or aspirants but still warranted Christ's direct intervention in their lives. Many who have had this experience did not previously believe in Christ, but they certainly did afterwards. Often, they turn to Christ for the rest of their life based upon the experience they had with Him, which can never be marginalized. Many times, these encounters involved Christ 'saving their life.' After such a conversion based upon direct experience, faith is not based upon believing in the unseen, but in the seen.

Having interviewed many people who have had this experience, certain common descriptions arise. Frequently, the person is alone and experiencing the deepest despair of their entire life. All hope is gone, and the person feels overwhelmed by forces outside of themselves that they cannot control. They see no logic in going on because they have no experience or proof of God and therefore the question of life after death is not a consideration. Fear of the future paralyzes their actions. Nothing brings joy, and depression and suicidal thoughts are prevalent. All light of soul is fading, and the abyss of nothingness becomes the looming dread of the soul. The person is not usually praying to any god or asking for help, and often does not have any religious affiliations.

Then something happens, and the person begins to feel like they have never felt before and something is coming towards them. All fear dissipates as the approach of this 'being' starts to fill the room. Soon, a liquid light floods their space with living fire and unimaginable brilliance, the like of which they have never imagined before. As warm, comforting light fills the space it drives away darkness and all unclean aspects of the environment and the soul. The person begins to feel that 'living love' now approaches them. They are so humbled that they 'fall down' in a sense of unworthiness and cannot look directly at the brilliance. The light and love come and 'hover' over the person and eventually touches them on the head or heart and fills their body, soul, and spirit with the grace and mercy of God. The person is cleansed and healed. Tremendous gratitude, faith, and conviction fill the person and they become filled with the fire of the spirit. The being tells them to rise. Once they are upon their feet, the being announces that His name is Christ, the Cosmic and Human 'I Am.' The person knows that the same Christ outside of them is now inside of them, and from that moment on they are wed to Christ.

After an experience of the Etheric Christ, the witness often becomes a devout believer in Christ and studies to try and understand what happened to them. Paul was knocked to the ground on the road to Damascus and blinded by the light of the Etheric Christ and then had to go into Damascus and wait in silence. Ananias was told by God to go to Paul and heal his blindness and teach him about the true nature of Christ and His teachings. Paul believed he had a direct revelation of Christ who continued to teach him long after the event. An effects of an experience of the Etheric Christ could last for a lifetime and may need the help of others to comprehend the experience. Paul was blind for three days and could not eat or drink afterwards until Ananias laid his hands upon his head and healed him through the power of Christ. Then, he taught Paul what he needed to know in order to come out of the darkness and into the wisdom, light, and love of Christ that he had experienced firsthand on the road to Damascus.

There seems to be at least three different ways to experience Christ in the etheric realm in modern times, what is called witnessing the Second Coming of Christ. One is the path just described, where Christ choses to appear to someone without their understanding why. He comforts them and they subsequently follow Him for the rest of their life with great fervor. This could be looked at as an experience that motivates the person's willpower. The willpower of the person might be exhausted, in danger, or at its end; then, Christ appears and regenerates the person's willpower and aligns it with His own divine will. Thus, the will of the divine intervenes and creates an initiation that did not require the usual training in thinking and the years of preparation of the aspirant's feelings that accompany initiation. Christ simply intervenes with His grace and mercy and claims the soul as His own.

The second type of experience with Christ is a subtle knowing that Dr. Steiner described as a 'feeling of being surrounded by Christ as our guide and leader.' This feeling is not a consciously developed cosmology derived through initiation knowledge. It is akin to the feeling that modern people have about the Earth being identified as a Being called Gaea. Christ is the comforter of the soul and can convey profound divine mercy without accompanying cosmological thinking or requiring years of abstinence, purification, devotion, and spiritual practice. This type of experience of Christ is not established in Christ-centered cosmology or the ritual practices of spiritual development. It is a feeling that knows that Christ is right and correct, though the person having this feeling may not be able to articulate why. This is evidenced in the millions of people who have a 'personal' relationship to Christ as their Savior. This type of Second Coming of Christ is a subtle feeling that their personal messiah is Christ who is always available to them as a friend, savior, guide, and 'Lord of their life.' This type of feeling experience of Christ in the Etheric Realm is a 'feeling of faith,' that is deeply 'known' in the heart of the Christian who arrives at this feeling without direct knowledge or experience. This is a common religious experience for many Christians who want to surrender their soul to the grace and mercy of the divine.

The path of 'feeling' Christ in the etheric can lead to less defined and understood aspects of the spiritual path, with many possible byways that can produce extreme emotional expression. A reverent feeling is a good beginning that should be followed up with daily spiritual practice and moral deeds, just as Paul had to have Ananias teach him about the true nature of Christ after the Damascus Event. The feeling path can often lead to giving away the direction of your spiritual path to a teacher, priest, guru, or another. The development of our higher capacities is incumbent upon our self, not others. We develop spiritually by taking independent steps through our own volition and willpower that are consciously created and directed by moral intent. The development of human free will is the aim of spiritual training. Vague feelings are fine as a beginning but disciplined, rhythmic communion with the divine is necessary to be able to rise into the etheric realm to see Christ in His Second Coming through consciously directed supersensible perception.

The gradual path to seeing Christ in the etheric is through first developing thinking, feeling, and willing into new capacities of soul, new supersensible organs that can see, hear, and communicate with the spiritual world. This path of development is steady, gradual, and step by step. To visualize, invoke, and embody Sophia, the Wisdom of the Cosmic Christ, is a sure way up the holy mountain. This type of angelic worship, emulation, effectively develops thinking into Moral Imagination, or warmed-up thoughts. Moral Imaginations are alive and connect the aspirant to other living archetypes of similar natures. They demonstrate their 'beingness' through direct communication, a dialogue in the Language of the Spirit. Moral Imaginations become the doorway to seeing into the etheric realm. But first, the astral body must be tamed and brought under the direct control of higher spiritual thoughts. The tamed astral body provides the fire of desire that enkindles awe, reverence, and devotion towards the divine and the desire for enlightenment for the sake of all sentient beings. This tamed fire warms morally spiritual thinking into fiery, living, Moral Imaginations that bring nourishment to the spiritual world, and then subsequently, nourishment to the aspirant from the nectar and ambrosia of the spiritual world. Symbiotic spiritual nourishment is the result of Moral Imaginations alighting in the soul from the spirit world.

Seeing Christ in the etheric, by any of the three ways described above, is seeing Christ in living Moral Imaginations. The purified etheric body can be the organ of perception of this cosmic light. The aspirant can train the mind to receive these Moral Imaginations by meditating on sense-free qualities of the spirit; like, the Seven Heavenly Virtues (humility, love, purity, gratitude, temperance, patience, diligence). Through development of a comprehensive spiritual cosmology, the aspirant can exercise the supersensible organ of vision by thinking about the invisible spiritual world and the beings who inhabit that world. Envisioning the workings of the spiritual hierarchies is one of the best ways to see the forces of life that are commonly thought of as invisible. Enough meditation and thinking about spiritual matters will eventually bring those realms into the purview of the aspirant. Angels have little to do with anything visible, but they can be imagined in ways that bring them into view.

The astral body may appear as visual images in the astral light; whereas, the etheric body manifests as music called the harmony of the spheres; and the physical body incarnates through the Language of the Spirit. Sight, sound, and the spoken word are transformed into thinking, feeling, and willing. We can see our thoughts, we can hear our feelings, and we can listen to our will. We need to be able to see, hear, and speak with Christ in the etheric realm to witness His etheric Second Coming.

Christ is in the etheric realm and most aspirants are working on their astral body, which separates them from the Christ. The desire body, astral body, is represented as the domain of Lucifer, the being of fallen light. Lucifer stands between the aspirant and the vision of Christ in the etheric. It takes a mental shock, an undefeatable feeling, or the conscious path of self-development to get through Lucifer to see Christ in the etheric realms. Lucifer keeps tempting the human's astral body until humility is sometimes difficult or impossible to achieve. The human 'I Am' needs to be egotistic up until age twenty-eight; but after that, it is selflessness that should prevail. Selfish pursuits are luciferic parts of our soul tempting us to be King of our own world. This type of pride will hinder experiencing the living nature of the etheric realms, and Christ's presence in those worlds.

The etheric body of Earth and the human etheric body are ruled by rhythm. Our breath and heartbeat are two examples of cosmic timing that we only partially control. In sleep, we have no control over those rhythms, and they reset to the universal rhythm of four heart beats to one breath once we go into deep sleep. These cosmic rhythms accompany our life and are created by a type of sound. Rhythm is the tool of the spirit that brings life and health. When natural rhythms are disturbed, the human body falls ill. We were somewhat asleep in the Garden of Eden, and we were healthy and without illness. When we awoke to the outside world, the forces of dissonance brought illness. When we take on unnatural rhythms in our life, they will deaden our etheric bodies. The initiate builds into their life healthy rhythms that nourish the etheric body to become a tool for supersensible spiritual perception. Christ feeds the initiate through the life of the etheric body and its healthy rhythms.

The being referred to as Ahriman is the lord of anti-thinking that darkens human thinking with grey shadow thoughts that are like spider webs entangling the mind. Ahriman is an arrhythmic assault on the etheric body. Once Ahriman can turn the rhythms and habits of an individual towards the dead and lifeless realms of evil machines, the etheric body begins to die. Ahriman loves death, fear, and cold-hearted hatred. It is Ahriman who uses 'spider-thoughts' as clever justification for a cosmology of entropy and mechanical nihilism. Ahriman and Lucifer cannot see Christ, but through their inherent nature they fight against Him without knowing. Neither one can see the middle ground where Christ lives. Neither one has the wisdom to understand Christ's love and sacrifice for humanity. Ahriman wants to kill the etheric body of the Earth and has done a pretty good job of it. He also wants to destroy the heart's ability to love and enflame the spirit. Ahriman wants everything to slow down to a cold, meaningless death. Lucifer wants the world to burn down completely in one great megalomaniacal act of conflagration.

To find Christ in the etheric realm, the aspirant on the path of self-initiation will first need to conquer the dragon of her astral desires and develop higher forms of Moral Imagination to approach Christ in the etheric through the Language of the Spirit. Through rhythmic spiritual practices, the etheric realm will begin to enliven thinking until it is full of warmth and the light of wisdom. Then, the aspirant can find Christ in His Second Coming, long before death and without an apocalypse in the outer world. Revelation and apocalypse come into the soul of the aspirant as the threshold to the spiritual world is crossed and the images of ascension appear before the spiritual soul. These images are the limits of the spiritual body of the aspirant arising through the intervention of Sophia and Christ in the etheric realm. The etheric realm holds the knowledge of the past, present, and future karma of the individual and the world. It is ever alive in renewing everything. The etheric body is, essentially, a complete picture of the Universe from beginning to end as an ever present 'now' rushing in from the future. Christ has claimed the etheric realm for humanity and thereby has assured a future where love and wisdom will reign.

The ongoing battle for the etheric realms (Earth and human) is the battle between Ahriman and Christ in our time. Ahriman is trying to crucify Christ in the etheric realm around the Earth, and in the human etheric body. Lucifer should have already been tamed in the astral body of the aspirant and turned into a healthy rhythmic force through the intervention of the Holy Spirit and Holy Sophia by undaunting spiritual practice. The intervention of the Holy Spirit with the Apostles created a World Pentecost or baptism by fire. The tongues of flame were the sign that the Apostles and the three Marys had tamed their astral bodies and learned to speak as Angels in a Language of the Spirit that everyone could understand simultaneously in their own tongue.

The spiritual training of the etheric body is much more difficult than taming the astral body of desires. The habits and rituals of life create the etheric body's relationship to the spirit and to matter. Most people spend their time thinking and acting exclusively in the material realm. The initiate, on the other hand, spends more time focused on, and thinking about, the spiritual realms. The daily spiritual practice of an initiate is more important to them than things in the outer world of material substances. Human and spiritual relationships are much more important for advancement than material things. The rhythms of synchronicity and spiritual manifestation begin to 'sound' in the initiate and becomes impressed in the etheric body over time, if the impulses come from the spiritual world instead of the physical world. The etheric body becomes the musical instrument of the initiate and living sound is heard as the initiate ascends to the super-etheric body around the Earth. The music of the spheres sounds in the etheric body and brings the forces and rhythms of the planets to the organs and systems of the human body. The planets and stars sing forth continuously as the etheric body answers in resonance. Both are mirrors of the divine plan that is like a grand symphony in which we play our humble instrument.

Experiencing Christ in the etheric is accompanied by heavenly sights, sounds, and words. We learn that sights denote the astral, sounds denote the etheric, and words denote the physical. Christ has already redeemed the physical nature of the Earth and humanity by the Mystery of Golgotha—His life, death, and resurrection. Christ is known as the 'Word' or 'Logos,' indicating that He is the Word of God that sounded forth creation as a spoken Language of the Spirit. The human body is a manifestation of the Word of God, the Temple of Wisdom. Christ descended from the Holy Trinity into a human body so that He could make humans whole and complete through His spiritual deeds; so that they might become a suitable vessel for the spirit.

The human physical body is the 'Word made flesh.' Through the three Pre-Earthly Deeds of Christ, humans became able to stand erect, speak, and think. Christ also brought with Him to Earth the human Ego capacity to think as a free being and donated the personal 'I Am' to each human being as His Fourth Deed. In our time, Christ's Fifth Deed is the renewing and redemption of the etheric bodies of humans, and the Earth, so that they will continue to have life. In the future, Christ will redeem the human astral body and Ego ('I Am') as His Sixth and Seventh Deeds as He continues to support humanity's spiritual evolution. Christ is found intimately in every part of the human physical constitution because He is the divine archetype of the human being who has donated, and subsequently redeemed, the human physical and etheric bodies, and will redeem the astral body and Ego in the future.

At this time, Christ is active in the etheric realms bringing the living forces of His resurrection body into these kingdoms. Christ brings the warmth, light, and levity to counteract the cold darkness of Ahrimanic gravity. The human soul stands in the middle of the battle, and much will be lost in both the Earthly and human etheric realms if the Wisdom of Christ is not understood. An initiate can receive the forces of the risen Christ and remake their personal etheric body into the image of Christ's etheric body, thus assuring eternal life. This is the future path of all faithful followers of Christ.

The etheric realm is the realm of time. Christ rules time and is the Lord of karma, destiny, and providence. If Christ cannot win the battle for life in the etheric, the Earth will change its destiny and destroy itself completely. The same is true for each individual who can either kill or enliven their own etheric body of formative forces. The aspirant can choose between the life and love of Christ or the selfish egotism and lies of Lucifer and the cold, dead nihilism of Ahriman, the Lord of Materialism. Lucifer distracts the aspirant from the true light while Ahriman darkens and extinguishes the light.

There is one more group of evil beings that are seldom spoken of that are called Asuras. These Asuric beings are led by the Anti-Christ Sorat (also Sorath), the Sun Demon. He is not well known in history and will unfold his full power in the future. His minions attack the human physical body and try to completely annihilate it for all time to come. They eat the human soul and wish to consume the inner flame in the human heart. They are equally cruel and hateful as the ahrimanic beings who also use drugs, addiction, sexual aberrations, and violence as their tools. They run rampant in Western society, and they present unsolvable questions of immorality and evil as they overwhelm the unprepared aspirant.

Christ battles Ahriman and Lucifer with the help of Sophia, Archai Michael, and the heavenly hosts. Sophia Christos, (Wisdom of the Cosmic Christ) battles against these beings in favor of humanity's appropriate spiritual development. Many humans are unaware that such realities build their world and that their every action helps one side or the other. Initiates sleep very little at night for knowing of this battle and the work to be done to combat evil. The uninitiated remain asleep while evil beings consume them with every act of vice and sin. They do not know of the War in Heaven that has come down to Earth, and are oblivious to the costs as they enjoy another hedonistic delight, acting as if there is no tomorrow and no spiritual world watching. At night, these souls have virtually nothing to offer the spiritual world as nourishment gleaned from the physical world and raised to the spiritual. Christ fights for each of these souls as a father would do for his child.

The landscape of the etheric body of the human being is the domain in which each person can make a difference, for better or for worse. Christ, and the entire spiritual world, stand ready to help the aspirant take each new step towards the divine. But it is still the free deed of the aspirant that either builds or destroys their personal etheric body. As for the etheric body of the Earth, suffice it to say that that battle is quite visible and heated. The greedy appear to be winning at this point because the Earth's life-body has suffered great damage. Consciousness is being raised slowly to focus on environmental homeostasis, at least as platitudes. The call to save Mother Earth has been heard and we will see who wins the battle. All of our lives are ultimately connected to that global battle for a living Earth. Inner and outer etheric awareness is crucial for the continuity of life on Earth and in the human body. Christ brings life, whereas Lucifer, Ahriman, and the Asuras bring death.

As we behold Christ's Seven Deeds to heal human evolution from the onslaught of evil, we are struck with awe, reverence, and wonder at the Divine Plan. The intricate design of Christ's Wisdom, manifesting through Love, is wondrous to contemplate. Christ's Divine Deeds for humanity are miraculous and He continues His loving offerings to vouchsafe humanity's future. Knowledge of Christ's Seven Deeds forges the initiate's fiery spiritual resolve to accomplish moral, conscientious deeds as Christ has demonstrated by His Deeds. Christ's Deeds are a type of spiritual nourishment that engender further spiritual deeds from humans that feed the divine world. The great mystery of the Second Coming of the Etheric Christ is the wonder of our age. Christ's Seven Cosmic Deeds span the entire spiritual evolution of humans becoming Angels and demonstrates that Christ will be with us until the end of time.

To behold the etheric realm of the Earth is to lift the veil of Isis/Sophia and witness Christ's Second Coming in the Etheric Realm. This is also a sign of the resurrection of Sophia from the darkness of history. As the Wisdom of Sophia is added to a picture of a living Earth, science gets the chance to re-think what life is really based upon. New discoveries are happening every day that reveal another living, intelligent aspect of Nature. Everywhere, Sophia is alive and inspiring the world. Sophia brings to us the Wisdom of the Cosmic Christ that is necessary to fully understand the Mystery of Golgotha and the Mystery of the Etheric Christ, the Second Coming of Christ in the Etheric Realm. This Wisdom is called by Rudolf Steiner, Sophia Christos the Wisdom of Christ. Christ is Love acting throughout all time, while Sophia is the Wisdom of Universal space. Together, they create cosmic awareness of the past, present, and future as the manifestation of Wisdom and Love. They are the new Alpha and the Omega.

The Mysteries of the Etheric Christ are the most personal and profound mysteries of the human being. Evolution hangs in the balance as the human soul life is fought over by good and evil beings. Each day is a battle in this war and each person, and humanity as a whole, is in danger of dying to the spirit. If this happens, it will darken the etheric realm and the spiritual world. Each human holds a key to whether the battle will be won or lost. Each person will be called on to declare whose side they are on, and the fate of their soul and spirit hangs in the balance.

Joining together with Sophia, in all of Her many forms, is one way to rise-up to the refined realms of the super-etheric where we can meet the Etheric Christ in His Second Coming in the Etheric Realm. Sophia is our guide, and She teaches us the Wisdom we need to understand the Cosmic Nature of Christ and the Language of the Spirit that He speaks. As we combine our virtuous development and the fruits of the virtuous labors of Sophia with the risen One, the 'Christ in me,' we can rise into the higher realms and participate in the work of the divine. Sophia is our personal midwife in the process of spirit birth, and Christ is the being who gives us our higher self and allows the pure soul to wed the higher spirit nature. The soul filled with Wisdom/Sophia can then join with the Spirit of Love, Christ, to become Sophia Christos, our higher Spirit-Self married to our own Life-Spirit.

Rudolf Steiner's Indications

Search for the New Isis, the Divine Sophia: The Quest for the Isis-Sophia, **Rudolf Steiner, Lecture in Dornach, December 24, 1920, GA 202**

"We do not lack Christ; but the knowledge of Christ, the Sophia of Christ, the Isis of Christ is lacking. This is what we should engrave in our souls as a content of the mystery of Christmas."

"Just as the Egyptians looked from Osiris to Isis, so we must learn to look again to the new Isis, the Holy Sophia. Christ will appear again in his spiritual form during the course of the twentieth century, not through the arrival of external events alone; but because human beings find the power represented by the Holy Sophia."

The Birth of the Light of the Earth out of Christmas Darkness, **Rudolf Steiner, Berlin, December 24, 1912, GA 143**

"Wisdom is great, is valuable and beings cannot exist without wisdom, yet love is even greater. The power and the strength underpinning the world is vast and something without which the world cannot exist; but love is even mightier."

The Spiritual Hierarchies, Rudolf Steiner, Lecture VIII. Düsseldorf, April 17, 1909, GA 110

"You know that the first foundation for the Ego was prepared in old Lemuria, when the present Moon separated from the Earth."

The Reappearance of Christ in the Etheric, Rudolf Steiner, Lecture V, Stuttgart, March 6, 1910, GA 118

"Initiation, however, always led into that mysterious land, which is spoken of as a country that seemed to have vanished out of the sphere of human experience. It withdrew during Kali Yuga [3,101 BC-1899 AD; Diagram I]; but for those who had received initiation there was always the possibility of guiding their steps into it. The accounts of this ancient country are touching. It is the same land to which the initiates again and again repair in order to fetch from it the new streams and impulses for all that is to be given to humanity from century to century. Again and again those who stand in this relationship with the spiritual world enter this mysterious land, which is called Shambhala. It is the primal fountainhead, into which clairvoyant sight once reached but which withdrew during Kali Yuga. It is spoken of as one would speak of an ancient fairyland, one that will return, however, into the realm of human beings. There will be Shambhala again after Kali Yuga has run its course. Humanity, through normal human faculties, will again grow into the land of Shambhala, from which the initiates bring strength and wisdom for their mission. There is Shambhala; there was Shambhala; Shambhala will come to be again for humanity. Among the first visions that human beings will have when Shambhala shows itself again will be Christ in His etheric form. Humanity has no other leader than the Christ to take it into the land that Oriental writings declare to have vanished. Christ will lead humanity to Shambhala."

The Appearance of Christ in the Etheric, Rudolf Steiner, Lecture Karlsruhe, January 25, 1910, GA 118

"…Humanity is ripening toward a time when the influences of the spiritual world will be felt ever more widely. The tremendous occurrences of the coming period will be discernible in all worlds. Even the human beings between death and a new birth will have new experiences in the other world as a result of the new Christ event in the etheric world. Unless they have prepared themselves on Earth to do so, however, they will no more be able to understand these events than will the human beings now incarnated on earth; they must have prepared themselves rightly to receive the events of this important moment."

The Damascus Event as the Second Coming

The first chapter of the *Acts of the Apostles* describes Christ's Ascension: "and a cloud received him out of their sight." As the disciples were looking up, two Angels appeared and said, "the same Jesus, taken up from you into heaven, shall come again in the same way as you have seen him go." This cloud of ascension is the etheric realm of the Earth. A spirit-land of life.

Starting in 1910, Rudolf Steiner gave a series of lectures announcing the advent of Christ's appearance in the sphere of the Earth's etheric (life) body—essentially the Second Coming of Christ in the Etheric or the Land of Shamballa. This would begin around 1930 and continue for the next 2,500 years. At first, only a few people would be aware of this new Deed of Christ. In time, more and more people—regardless of their religious affiliations—will be enlightened by witnessing Christ's etheric manifestation as a living presence. Such Damascus Events are a birth of a new natural clairvoyance that will become the common experience of anyone who can look through the astral spiritualized fire and light at the miraculously divine Christ-light.

Another way to experience Christ manifesting in the etheric body of the Earth, and the human being's personal etheric body, is to encounter Christ as the Comforter. This has been documented many times in history when Christ Himself, appearing as a human being, walks into the room and provides comfort and healing. Rudolf Steiner describes this second type of meeting Christ in the etheric realm in the following words from *The Reappearance of Christ in the Etheric*, Rudolf Steiner, Lecture IX. *The Etherization of the Blood*, Basel October 1, 1911, GA 130:

> "The Christ will become a living comforter. Many a human being will have this experience when sitting silent in his room, heavy-hearted and oppressed, not knowing which way to turn. The door will open, and the Etheric Christ will appear and speak words of consolation to him. The Christ will become a living Comforter to humans. Many a time when people—even in considerable numbers—are sitting together, not knowing what to do, and waiting, they will see the Etheric Christ. He will Himself be there, will confer with them, will make His voice heard in such gatherings. These times are approaching, and this positive, constructive element will take real effect in the evolution of mankind."

The experience of Saul, who became Paul on the road to Damascus, can be experienced by other people since the 1930's and will continually increase in numbers for the next 2,500 years until it becomes a common experience for awakened souls. Paul experienced a blinding light and the voice of Christ speaking to him as he was knocked to the ground. He remained blind for days until Ananias came to heal him in the name of Christ Jesus. Paul experienced a sudden illumination like an initiation, and then became etherically clairvoyant afterwards and could see Christ as a living being in the realm of the etheric body of the Earth. This type of initiation can, in our day, happen at any moment to a person who desires to rise to spiritual realms. This experience of illumination awakens a new type of clairvoyance in the person having the spiritual vision that opens the 'spiritual eye' which can look into the heavenly world and bring forth the truth about the Living Cosmic Christ's appearance in the etheric realm.

The Damascus Event opens what Rudolf Steiner calls 'etheric vision,' which can witness Christ's Second Coming in the etheric realm (through the astral light) as an etheric Being of Light (Angels), Music (Archangels), and Word of Life (Archai). This perception of Christ in the etheric realm, is tantamount to the Second Coming of Christ in the etheric realm of the Earth and the human etheric body—called Shamballa in the Earth's etheric realm or the Temple of Wisdom in the human etheric body. Paul was the first person, who had not known Jesus directly, to experience Christ's Second Coming in the etheric and understand that Christ could now be directly witnessed in the etheric realm as a living Being. This experience was similar to Moses seeing God in the burning bush and was a type of revelation for Paul, like Saint John's revelation of the apocalypse, which is often seen as a description of the Second Coming of Christ.

Paul's initiation on the road to Damascus was the third initiation Saul/Paul had undergone in his life. He was very familiar with the Hebrew and Greek forms of initiation which prepared him for the new initiation of Christ. That is why Saul/Paul did not believe Jesus was the Messiah and why he persecuted the followers of Jesus of Nazareth. Paul had been taught that the great solar deity (Vishvakarman, Ahura Mazdao, the Word, the Logos) was in the spiritual world coming towards the Earth in the rays of the Sun, not incarnated on the Earth in a human body. But once Paul had received his initiation directly from Christ Jesus in a blinding flash, he could see that Christ had come down from the Sun and could now be seen in the aura of the Earth as Christ Jesus, the One who conquered death through His resurrection and ascension.

The mysterious super-etheric realm of life is called by Rudolf Steiner, the 'realm of spiritual economy', or the land of Shamballa, the etheric realm, the life body of the Earth, the human etheric body, the elemental kingdoms, elemental beings, and the etheric formative forces. These realms work through the ethers of warmth, light, sound, life, and akasha to bring about life on Earth.

Through Paul's Damascus Event, he gained 'etheric vision,' a new type of clairvoyance based upon seeing the etheric form of

Christ through the astral light. Once etheric vision is established, direct knowledge and contact with Christ is possible and a Language of the Spirit can be learned for communication and communion with Angels, Archangels, Archai, and Elohim. Each person has the possibility of meeting Christ in His etheric form as a personal Second Coming of Christ, a revelation and initiation that opens new supersensible organs of perception developing etheric clairvoyance.

Humanity will ascend to a cognition of the spiritual world in the near future and will see the physical world permeated by a new 'country,' or new realm—the etheric. Humanity's physical body will develop new organs of perception over the next 2,500 years through the addition of etheric clairvoyance; that indeed, is already here but which many will soon learn to develop. Christ came in the physical realm only once through the Mystery of Golgotha—the life, death, resurrection, and ascension of Jesus Christ. Now Christ comes to those who can rise-up to Him in the etheric realm. In the far future, Christ will also be found redeeming the astral realm of the Earth in the Sixth Cultural Epoch, the Russian/Slavic Age of Civilization that will be seeded by the Second Coming of Christ for the next 2,500 years. In that age, Christ will become a companion of the awakened ones and will walk beside them as a friend and guide.

Through the vision of the Damascus Event, a new clairvoyance is awakened that can see into the invisible lands that sustain life through etheric forces. These realms have been known for thousands of years as the Land of Shambhala, where the Temple of Wisdom can rejuvenate the masters and initiates who go there seeking Wisdom and Love from the Cosmic Christ and Sophia. This land was known by initiates of the past and, at one time, was much more accessible but has now been withdrawn from the sight of most humans. Shambhala, or New Jerusalem, can be entered today by those who, as initiates, go there from time to time to be strengthened and re-enlivened with courage and fortitude.

The Damascus Event as the Second Coming

Everyone in our time can develop the selfless wisdom, fiery love, and moral strength that it takes to make it to the Land of Shambhala, where the perfected bodies of all the saints, great teachers, buddhas and bodhisattvas exist in perfected archetypal forms that are models for striving humans to emulate. This realm is where the celestial 'mansions' of good souls are being built, with Christ as the foundation stone. This is the New Jerusalem that Saint John spoke about in his book of revelations that is built by the true believers who preach the Eternal Gospel and sing the New Song. Attaining Shambhala, witnessing the Second Coming, is the same as putting on your 'white tunic' and returning to your home at the foot of the Throne of the Divine as one of the chosen. This personal rising-up into the 'third heaven' can happen to anyone, at any time, if they have developed the moral and spiritual prerequisites. It can also happen when one of the faithful is about to lose hope and give up on life—then Christ walks in and dispels their fears and doubts and comforts them with His Wisdom and Love.

Part of the preparation for ascension into the etheric is a strengthening of clear consciousness and a sense of responsibility towards developing spiritual perception. Studying Spiritual Science will open the aspirant to the Language of the Spirit and help morally prepare him for developing the supersensible organs necessary to witness the living beings in the etheric realm and working throughout the human etheric body. With holy wonder for the many gifts, deeds, and sacrifices of Christ, awe for the divine creative power of the Father God, and reverence for the ever-present help of the spiritual world that comes from the Comforter, the Holy Spirit of Christ, and the Wisdom of Sophia, we have the ability in our time to rise to refined realms where life is burgeoning ever anew through the gifts of the spirit, truly a New Paradise descending from heaven. We too can attain the light of spiritual illumination which fell upon Paul/Saul during the Damascus Event that created the 'first witness' of the Second Coming of Christ in the Etheric and the revelation of Christ's newest Deed of redeeming the etheric life-forces of the Earth and humanity.

Rudolf Steiner on the Damascus Event

***The Christ Impulse and the Development of the Ego-Consciousness—Correspondences,* Rudolf Steiner, Lecture V, *Between the Microcosm and the Macrocosm,* Berlin, March 9, 1910 GA 116**

"That is true; it will return to earth! And the guide thereto will be He [Christ] Whom men will see, when, through the vision of the Event of Damascus, they reach the Land of Shamballa. 'Shamballa'—for so this Land is called—has withdrawn from the sight of man. It can only be entered today by those who, as Initiates, go there from time to time to be strengthened. The old forces can no longer lead man thither. That is why Eastern literature speaks with such tragic despair of the vanished Land of Shambhala. But the Christ-Event, which will be vouchsafed to man in this century through his newlyawakened faculties, will bring back the Fairy-Land of Shambhala, which through the whole of Kali-Yuga could only be known to the Initiates."

***The Christ Impulse and the Development of the Ego Consciousness,* Rudolf Steiner, Lecture IV, *The Sermon on the Mount,* Berlin, February 8, 1910, GA 116**

"Instead of acquiring clear notions of the fact that men must grow up as regards their capacities so that a great number, and finally all, might experience the Event of Damascus—that is: might experience the Christ in the atmosphere around the earth, and see Him in His etheric body—it was believed that Christ would descend again in a physical body, for the materialistic satisfaction of those who refuse to believe in the spirit, and who will not believe what St. Paul saw in the Event of Damascus: that Christ is in the Earth-atmosphere and that He is always there! 'I am with you always, even unto the end of the world!' Those who develop the methods of clairvoyant vision into the Spiritual world will find what, could not be found there in the pre-Christian time: the Christ in His etheric body. That is the important progress in the evolution of humanity; before the first half of our century has elapsed, those faculties by means of which the event of Damascus becomes a personal experience, will develop naturally as it were, and men will see the Christ in His etheric body. He will not descend into flesh, but man will ascend when he has acquired understanding of the spirit."

The Reappearance of Christ in the Etheric, **Rudolf Steiner, Lecture IX,** *The Etherization of the Blood,* **October 1, 1911, Basel, GA 130**

"Then in the course of the next three thousand years, He [Christ] will become visible to greater and greater numbers of people. This will inevitably come to pass in the natural course of development. A number of individuals will see the Etheric Christ and will themselves experience the event that took place at Damascus. But this will depend upon such men learning to be alert to the moment when Christ draws near to them. In only a few decades from now it will happen, particularly to those who are young— already preparation is being made for this—that some individual here or there has certain experiences. If he has sharpened his vision through having assimilated Anthroposophy, he may become aware that suddenly someone has come near to help him, to make him alert to this or that. The truth is that Christ has come to him, although he believes that what he saw is a physical man. He will come to realize that what he saw was a super-sensible being, because it immediately vanishes. Many a human being will have this experience when sitting silent in his room, heavy-hearted and oppressed, not knowing which way to turn. The door will open, and the Etheric Christ will appear and speak words of consolation to him. The Christ will become a living Comforter to men. However strange it may as yet seem, it is true nevertheless that many a time when people—even in considerable numbers—are sitting together, not knowing what to do, and waiting, they will see the Etheric Christ. He will Himself be there, will confer with them, will make His voice heard in such gatherings. These times are approaching, and the positive, constructive element now described will take real effect in the evolution of mankind."

True Nature of the Second Coming, Rudolf Steiner, Lecture I, *The Event of Christ's Appearance in the Etheric World*, Stuttgart, July 25, 1910, GA 118

"A man who was convinced with particular intensity through such perception, was Paul—in the vision at Damascus. But this etheric sight will develop in individual human beings as a natural faculty. In days to come it will be more and more possible for men to experience what Paul experienced at Damascus. We are now able to grasp quite a different aspect of Spiritual Science."

"And from this experience they will realize that this is the same Being who at the beginning of our era fulfilled the Mystery of Golgotha, that He is indeed the Christ. Just as Paul at Damascus was convinced at the time: This is Christ! ... so there will be men whose experiences in the etheric world will convince them that in very truth Christ lives. The supreme mystery of the age in which we are living is the Second Coming of Christ—that is its true nature."

The Reappearance of Christ in the Etheric, Rudolf Steiner, Lecture VIII, *The Return of Christ,* Palermo, April 18, 1910, GA 118

"All the faculties that today can be acquired by means of initiation will in the future be universal faculties of humanity. This condition of soul, this experiencing of soul, is called in esotericism the "Second Coming of Christ." Christ will not be incarnated again in a physical body, but He will appear in an etheric body as in the street near Damascus. Christ incarnated on the physical plane when humanity had become limited to the physical body."

True Nature of the Second Coming, Rudolf Steiner, Lecture I, *The Event of Christ's Appearance in the Etheric World,* Karlsruhe, July 25, GA 118

"When this is understood, Spiritual Science is disclosed as the means of preparing men to recognize the return of Christ, in order that it shall not be their misfortune to overlook this event but that they shall be mature enough to grasp the great happening of the Second Coming of Christ. Men will become capable of seeing etheric bodies and among them, too, the etheric body of Christ; that is to say, they will grow into a world where Christ will be revealed to their newly awakened faculties. There will be men whose experiences in the etheric world will convince them that in very truth Christ lives. The supreme mystery of the age in which we are living is the Second Coming of Christ. Just as other happenings preceded the Christ Event in Palestine, so will those who prophetically foretold His coming follow Him after the time referred to, after He Himself has become visible to mankind again in the etheric body. The preparers of His coming will be recognizable in a new form to men who have experienced the new Christ Event."

The Festivals and Their Meaning II: Easter, **Rudolf Steiner, Lecture I,** *Easter: the Festival of Warning,* **Dornach, April 2, 1920, GA 198**

"The writings of Paul, as we know them, convey only a weak reflection of all that he experienced inwardly. But even so, when he speaks of the event of Damascus, we can discern that he speaks as one who through this event attained knowledge of cosmic happenings lying behind the veil of the world of sense."

Inner Realities of Evolution, **Rudolf Steiner, Lecture V,** *Inner Aspect of the Earth-Embodiment of the Earth,* **Berlin, December 5, 1911, GA 132**

"…Among the many proofs of this fact which occult science is able to provide, is the following: That the event of Damascus will, in the course of the next three thousand years, as we have often said, be renewed for a sufficiently great number of mankind. This means, that capacities will be developed in man which will enable him to perceive the Christ as an etheric figure on the astral plane, as Paul saw Him on the road to Damascus…"

From Jesus to Christ, **Rudolf Steiner, Lecture X, Karlsruhe, October 14, 1911, GA 131**

"And in the next three thousand years the truth that Christ is acting as Karmic Judge will become apparent to a sufficiently large number of people. Christ Himself will be experienced by men as an etheric Form. Like Paul before Damascus, they will know quite intimately that Christ lives, and is the Source for the reawakening of the physical prototype we received at the beginning of our evolution, and need if the Ego is to attain full development."

The Reappearance of Christ in the Etheric, **Rudolf Steiner, Lecture VII,** *The Return of Christ*, **Palermo, April 18, 1910, GA 118**

"What Paul experienced at Damascus, which was a personal experience for him, will become common experience for a certain number of people. At the event of Damascus, he could say for the first time with his clairvoyant consciousness: Christ exists! The people who will experience the event of Damascus in the twentieth century will receive direct knowledge of Christ. Through this, the possibility is given that a certain number of human beings, and then more and more, shall experience during the next 2,500 years a repetition of the event of Damascus. The greatness and power of the next age will consist in the fact that for many people the event of Damascus will come to life; that through these faculties of which I have just spoken the Christ will become perceptible in the spiritual sphere of the earth."

The Christ Impulse and the Development of the Ego Consciousness, **Rudolf Steiner, Lecture VII,** *The Further Development of Conscience,* **Berlin, May 8, 1910, GA 116**

"As a parallel to the appearance of the Event of Damascus a great number of people in the course of the twentieth century will experience something like the following: As soon as they have acted in some way, they will learn to contemplate their deed; they will become more thoughtful, they will have an inner picture of the deed."

Rosicrucian Esotericism, **Rudolf Steiner, Lecture IX,** *Man's Experience after Death,* **Budapest, June 11, 1909, GA 109**

"Saul who, as an initiate of the Jewish Mysteries, knew full well that the "Great Aura," Ahura Mazdao, would one day unite with the earth, rebelled against the belief that this being could have died on the shameful cross. Although he had participated in the events in Palestine, he did not believe that this great spirit had dwelt on the earth in Jesus of Nazareth. It was when he became clairvoyant near the gates of Damascus that in the earth's aura he beheld the Christ spirit, the living Christ, who could not previously have been seen there."

The Principle of Spiritual Economy, **Rudolf Steiner, Lecture V,** *Results of Spiritual Scientific Investigations of the Evolution of Humanity:* **II, Rome, March 31, 1909, GA 111**

"We see the first example of this in Saul when he became Paul. What happened to him on his way to Damascus must be interpreted as something similar to an initiation. The reason that he needed only a few minutes for it was that he had attained a certain maturity in the preceding life."

From Jesus to Christ, Rudolf Steiner, Lecture VI, *St. John and St. Paul, First Adam and Second Adam*, Karlsruhe, October 10, 1911, GA 131

"Christ had appeared to the disciples also; Paul refers to that, and the events lived through with the Risen One were the same for Paul as they had been for the disciples. But what Paul immediately joins to these, as the outcome for him of the event of Damascus, is his wonderful and easily comprehensible theory of the Being of Christ. What, from the event of Damascus onwards, was the Being of Christ for Paul? The Being of Christ was for him the 'Second Adam'; and he immediately differentiates between the first Adam and the second Adam, the Christ."

On the Fifth Gospel, Rudolf Steiner, Lecture X, Berlin, January 13, 1914, GA 148

"Paul realizes now that formerly he had seen Christ while He was still in the spiritual world. The Event at Damascus had revealed to him Christ had now passed into the Aura of the Earth and was living in the Aura of the Earth. That is the great truth concerning which so many who lived in the early centuries of Christianity uttered such strange words."

Esoteric Christianity and the Mission of Christian Rosenkreutz, Rudolf Steiner, Lecture IV, *Rosicrucian Christianity,* Lecture II, Neuchatel, September 28, 1911, GA 130

"...Then, in the future, although it will only happen to a small number of people to begin with, they will be able to experience Paul's vision on the road to Damascus and to perceive the Etheric Christ, who will come among men in super-sensible form. But before this happens man will have to return to a spiritual view of nature... "

"And in the course of the next three thousand years this will become possible because it will no longer be necessary to teach from documents, for through the beholding of Christ human beings will themselves learn to understand the experience Paul had on the way to Damascus. Mankind itself will pass through the experience of Paul."

"The Maitreya Buddha will appear five thousand years after Buddha was enlightened under the bodhi tree, that is, about three thousand years from now. [Diagram III] He will be the successor of Gautama Buddha. Among true occultists this is no longer in doubt. Occultists of both the West and the East are in agreement about it. So, two things are beyond question: Firstly, that the Christ could appear only once in a physical body; secondly that He will appear in the twentieth century in etheric form. Great individualities will certainly appear in the twentieth century, like the Bodhisattva, the successor of Gautama Buddha, who will become the Maitreya Buddha in about three thousand years. But no true occultist will give to any human being physically incarnated in the twentieth century the name of Christ, and no real occultist will expect the Christ in the physical body in the twentieth century. Every genuine occultist would find such a statement erroneous. The Bodhisattva, however, will especially point to the Christ."

***Excursus on the Gospel According to St. Mark*, Rudolf Steiner, Lecture IV, *Excursus*, Berling, January 16, 1911, GA 124.**

"Men had now to understand what Paul taught to all, what it was that all men could receive into them through the revelation of Damascus. Although this event is described in the Bible as a sudden illumination, yet those who know the truth regarding such occurrences know that it can happen at any moment to one who desires to rise to spiritual realms; and that through what such a man experiences he becomes a changed Being."

***From Jesus to Christ*, Rudolf Steiner, Lecture VIII, *The Two Jesus Children, Zoroaster and Buddha*, Karlsruhe, October 12, 1911, GA 131**

"What Paul experienced on the road to Damascus was something which he knew could be experienced only when the Scriptures were fulfilled; when a perfect human Phantom, a human body risen from the grave in a super-sensible form, would appear in the spiritual atmosphere of the earth. And that is what he saw! That is what appeared to him on the road to Damascus and left him with the conviction: 'He was there—He is risen! For what is there could come only from Him: it is the Phantom which can be seen by all human individualities who seek to relate themselves to the Christ.'"

The Festivals and Their Meaning II: Easter, Rudolf Steiner, Lecture VIII, *Spiritual Bells of Easter, Spiritual Bells of Easter,* Pt. II, Cologne, April 11, 1909, GA 109

"It was seen again when the eyes of Saul, illumined by clairvoyance on the road to Damascus, beheld and recognized in the radiance of heavenly fire the One Who had fulfilled the Mystery of Golgotha. And so, both Moses and Paul beheld the Christ: Moses beheld Him in the material fire in the burning thornbush and in the lightning on Sinai, but only inwardly could he be made aware that it was the Christ Who spoke with him."

The Principle of Spiritual Economy, Rudolf Steiner, Lecture VIII, *The Event of Golgotha. The Brotherhood of the Holy Grail. The Spiritualized Fire,* Cologne, April 11, 1909, GA 109

"It was perceived again when Saul opened his eyes on his way to Damascus, found that they had become illumined and clairvoyant, and recognized in the heavenly fire the One who had accomplished the Mystery of Golgotha. Both Saul, who became Paul, and Moses saw the Christ. Moses saw Him in the material fire—in the burning thornbush and in the lightning fire on Sinai—and only his inner being could tell him that the Christ spoke to him. On the other hand, Christ appeared to the enlightened eye of Paul from the spiritual and etherealized fire. Just as matter and spirit stand in a relationship to one another in the evolution of the world, there exists also in the course of the world a relationship between the mysterious fire of the bramble-bush and of Sinai on the one hand, and the wondrous apparition of Saul on the other—that is, the fire that shines brightly to him from the clouds and transforms him into Paul."

***The Spiritual Guidance of the Individual and Humanity*,
Rudolf Steiner, Appendix: *The Mission of the New Revelation
of the Spirit*, Copenhagen, June 5, 1911, GA 15**

"…As I have pointed out frequently, the experience of the impulse of the Christ event that Paul, an individual filled with grace, had on the road to Damascus will eventually become the common property of all human beings. As Paul knew through a spiritual revelation who Christ was and what he had done, so all people will eventually receive this knowledge, this vision. We are at the threshold of the age when many people will experience a renewal of the Christ event of St. Paul. It is an intrinsic part of the evolution of our earth that many people will experience for themselves the spiritual vision, the spiritual eye, that opened up for Paul on the road to Damascus. This spiritual eye looks into the spiritual world, bringing us the truth about Christ, which Paul had not believed when he had heard it in Jerusalem. The occurrence of this event is a historical necessity."

***The Festivals and Their Meaning*, Rudolf Steiner, Lecture III, *Ascension and Pentecost—World-Pentecost: The Message of Anthroposophy*, Christiana, May 17, 1923**

"Thus, in the light of Spiritual Science, the Pentecost secret reveals to us that the Mystery of Golgotha has replaced the Sun-Myth of the ancient Mysteries. It was Paul who, through the revelation that came to him at Damascus, realized with particular clarity that Christ was the Sun-Being. Through the revelation at Damascus Paul realized that without being transported into the spiritual world, man can behold the Christ, and therefore that He had in very truth descended to the earth. From this moment he knew that the disciples of Christ Jesus spoke the truth; for the sublime Sun-Being had now come down from the heavens to the earth."

The Reappearance of Christ in the Etheric, Rudolf Steiner, Lecture III, *The Sermon on the Mount,* Munchen, March 15, 1910, GA 118

"Before the first half of the twentieth century has passed, some people will, with full I-consciousness, experience the penetration of the divine-spiritual world into the physical, sensible world in the same way as Saul did during his transformation into Paul before Damascus. This will then become the normal condition for a number of people. Christ will not incarnate again in a physical body as He did at that time in Jesus; nothing would be achieved by it now. From the middle of the twentieth century on, and continuing for the next 2,500 years, this will happen more and more often. Enough people will by then have experienced the event at Damascus that it will be taken as a common occurrence on the earth. We occupy ourselves with Spiritual Science so that these newly appearing faculties, which are at first barely perceptible, may not be overlooked and lost to humanity and that those blessed with this new power of vision may not be considered dreamers and fools but may instead have the support and understanding of a small group of people who in their common purpose may prevent these delicate soul seeds and soul qualities from being roughly trampled to death for lack of human understanding."

The Principle of Spiritual Economy, **Rudolf Steiner, Lecture III,** ***Christianity in Human Evolution, Leading Individualities and Avatar Beings,*** **Berlin, February,15, 1909, GA 109**

"People like these were especially common in European countries, and they had always been able to experience inwardly in miniature a kind of Pauline revelation, that is the experience through which Saul became Paul on the road to Damascus. It was possible because the multiplied copies of the etheric body of Jesus of Nazareth had been preserved and were in these centuries woven into the etheric bodies of a large number of people who wore these multiplied copies as one would wear a garment."

The Gospel of St. John in Relation to the Other Three Gospels, **Rudolf Steiner, Lecture XIII,** ***The Cosmic Significance of the Mystery of Golgotha,*** **Kassel, July 6, 1909, GA 112**

"And men will further learn to grasp the fact that through the deed of Golgotha, not only was it revealed to human cognition that death is in reality the source of life, but man was provided with an attitude toward death which permitted him to infuse more and more life into his own being, until ultimately it will become wholly alive—that is, until he will be able to rise from all death, until he has overcome death. That is what was revealed to Paul when he saw the living Christ on the road to Damascus—when he knew: Christ liveth—as he gazed with his newly found clairvoyance into what constituted the environment of the earth. As an Old-Testament initiate he knew that until then the earth had lacked a certain light, but now he saw that light in it; hence the Christ was present; hence also, He Who had hung on the

Cross was the Christ in Jesus of Nazareth. Thus, there came to Paul, on the road to Damascus, an understanding of what had taken place on Golgotha."

Planetary Spheres and Their Influence on Mans Life on Earth and in the Spiritual Worlds, **Rudolf Steiner, Lecture I,** ***The Threefold Sun and the Risen Christ,*** **London, April 24, 1922, GA 211**

"And this secret, that the Gods too undergo evolution—this secret Christ communicated to His initiate pupils after His Resurrection. This secret Paul also learned through the natural initiation that he experienced outside Damascus. What stunned and shook Paul to the depths of his being was the knowledge that the Power that had formerly been sought in the Sun had now become united with the powers of Earth. But when Paul received enlightenment on his way to Damascus, at that moment he knew that it was he himself who had been mistaken, in that he was ready to believe only what had hitherto been true. For now, he saw that what had been true, had become changed; the Being Who dwelt formerly only in the Sun had now descended to Earth and continued to live in the forces of the Earth."

The Festivals and Their Meaning: Ascension and Pentecost, **Rudolf Steiner, Lecture II,** ***Whitsun: The Festival of the Free Individuality,*** **Hamberg, May 15, 1910, GA 118**

"We know that we live in an important time of human evolution: that already before the close of this century new forces will develop in the human soul which will lead man to the unfolding of a kind of etheric clairvoyance, whereby, as if through a natural development, there will be renewed for certain human beings the event which Paul experienced at Damascus; and that in this way, for the heightened spiritual powers of man, Christ will return in an etheric garb. Ever more and more souls will share in what Paul experienced at Damascus. Then it will be seen in the world that Spiritual Science is the revelation, heralding a renewed and transformed truth of the Christ Impulse."

From Jesus to Christ, **Rudolf Steiner, Lecture VIII. Karlsruhe October 12, 1911, GA 131**

"But what was it that convinced Paul? In a certain sense Paul was an Initiate before the Event of Damascus. His Initiation had combined the ancient Hebrew principle and the Greek principle. He knew that an Initiate became, in his etheric body, independent of the physical body, and could appear in the purest form of his etheric body to those who were capable of seeing it. If Paul had had the vision of a pure etheric body, independent of a physical body, he would have spoken differently. He would have said that he had seen someone who had been initiated and would be living on further in the course of earth evolution, independently of the physical body. He would not have found this particularly surprising. What Paul experienced on the road to Damascus could not have been that. He had experienced something which he knew could be experienced only when the Scriptures were fulfilled; when a perfect human Phantom, a human body risen from the grave in a super-sensible form, would appear in the spiritual atmosphere of the earth. And that is what he saw! That is what appeared to him on the road to Damascus and left him with the conviction: 'He was there—He is risen! For what is there could come only from Him: it is the Phantom which can be seen by all human individualities who seek to relate themselves to the Christ.' This is what convinced him that Christ was already there; that he would not come first in the future, but was actually present there in a physical body, and that this physical body had rescued the primal form of the human physical body for the salvation of all men."

"The Damascus Event opened for Paul what Rudolf Steiner calls "etheric vision"; through which one can witness the Christ's Second Coming in the etheric realm (through the astral light) as an etheric Being of Light (Angels), Music (Archangels), and Word of Life (Archai). This perception of Christ in the etheric realm, is tantamount to the Second Coming of Christ in the etheric realm of the Earth and the human etheric body—called Shambhala in the Earth's etheric realm or the Temple of Wisdom in the human etheric body. Paul was the first person, who had not known Jesus directly, to experience Christ's Second Coming in the etheric and understand that Christ could now be directly witnessed in the etheric realm as a living Being. This experience was similar to Moses seeing God in the burning bush and was a type of revelation for Paul, like Saint John's revelation of the apocalypse, which is often seen as a description of the Second Coming of Christ."

"Paul's initiation on the road to Damascus was the third initiation Saul/Paul had undergone in his life. He was very familiar with the Hebrew and Greek forms of initiation which prepared him for the new initiation of Christ. That is why Saul/Paul did not believe Jesus was the Messiah and why he persecuted the followers of Jesus of Nazareth. Paul had been taught that the great solar deity (Vishvakarman, Ahura Mazdao, the Word, the Logos) was in the spiritual world coming towards the Earth in the rays of the Sun, not incarnated on the Earth in a human body. But once Paul had received his initiation directly from Christ Jesus in a blinding flash, he could see that Christ had come down from the Sun and could now be seen in the aura of the Earth as Christ Jesus, the One who conquered death through His resurrection and ascension."

Rosicrucian Esotericism, **Rudolf Steiner, Lecture IX.**
Man's Experience after Death, **Budapest, June 11, 1909, GA 109**

"A clairvoyant, living before the event of Golgotha, would not have seen in the Earth's aura what could be seen there later on, when Christ Jesus had passed through the death on Golgotha. Let us now think of the event of Damascus. Saul who, as an initiate of the Jewish Mysteries, knew full well that the 'Great Aura,' Ahura Mazdao, would one day unite with the Earth, rebelled against the belief that this being could have died on the shameful cross."

"It was when he became clairvoyant near the gates of Damascus that in the Earth's aura he beheld the Christ spirit, the living Christ, who could not previously have been seen there."

True Nature of the Second Coming, **Rudolf Steiner, Lecture II,**
The Second Coming of Christ in the Etheric World, **Stuttgart, July 25, 1910, GA 118**

"It is spoken of as one would speak of an ancient fairyland, one that will return, however, into the realm of human beings. There will be Shambhala again after Kali Yuga has run its course.

Humanity, through normal human faculties, will again grow into the land of Shambhala, from which the initiates bring strength and wisdom for their mission. There is Shambhala; there was Shambhala; Shambhala will come to be again for humanity. Among the first visions that human beings will have when Shambhala shows itself again will be Christ in His etheric form."

"When once human beings are able to immerse their gaze into Shambhala, then only will they be able to understand various things that are indeed contained in the Gospels."

"Through Paul's Damascus Event, he gained this "etheric vision," as a new type of clairvoyance based upon seeing the etheric form of Christ through the astral light. Once etheric vision is established, direct knowledge and contact with Christ is possible and a Language of the Spirit, or 'Grail Language' can be learned that inscribes into the Akasha and serves for communication with those loved ones across the threshold, and for communion with Angels, Archangels, Archai, and Exusiai (Elohim, Spirits of Form). Each individual has the possibility of meeting Christ in His etheric form as a personal Second Coming of Christ, a revelation and initiation that opens new supersensible organs of perception developing etheric clairvoyance."

"Humanity will ascend to a cognition of the spiritual world in the near future and will see the physical world permeated by a new 'country,' or new realm—the etheric. Humanity's physical body will develop new organs of perception over the next 2,500 years through the addition of etheric clairvoyance; that indeed, is already here now but which many will soon learn to develop."

"The actual physical metamorphoses of the human brain that was needed in preparation for this new cognition to unfold in Archangelic Period of Michael (1,879-2,229 AD) was brought about for all human beings by the activities of the Archangel Gabriel during his rulership of the Archangelic Period of Gabriel (1,510-1,879 AD)."

Esoteric Lessons 1904-1909, **Rudolf Steiner, Lesson 49, Berlin, May 5, 1909, GA 266/1**

"Here we must remember that spiritual beings of various levels during various ages direct the destiny of the Earth. From approximately the fifteenth century onward the direction lay in the hands of that being whom we call the Archangel Gabriel. He had the task of correctly directing the births on Earth so that gradually among humans an organ was developed that is found in the frontal cavity above the root of the nose. It is not directly physically perceptible; however, if a corpse of today and a corpse from the 13th century, for example, were compared, differences in structure and the windings of the brain would be found at the location mentioned. This organ was gradually prepared by the Archangel Gabriel in humans so that they would be in a position to receive the message of [Archangel] Michael, who took over the regency from him in 1879."

"Michael will imprint the message of theosophy into the human being by means of this new organ; indeed, not directly, but in such a way that he lets his wisdom stream into the etheric bodies of humans through the Great White Lodge [Shambhala]. From there humans must send it consciously into the organ for this wisdom and then allow it to work in the etheric body."

"Gabriel worked [during his last regency] upon humans in the time from conception and birth. The human brain was different earlier; it always received, so to speak, fresh impulses. It no longer receives these. Instead of them it has the new organ, which humans must develop out of their own initiative. What happens to those who do not do this, who do not want to receive the message of the Archangel Michael? Those who make themselves receptive to it are ready to work in the right way on the evolution of the Earth and humanity. And esotericists should place this high, ideal goal before their soul in all modesty; but also, with determination and become constantly more conscious of their lofty task involving great responsibility. "The others who do not use their organ thereby cause it to dry up; because every organ that is not used degenerates. They thereby they avoid the work that they are supposed to do. This work will nevertheless be done; the Archangel Michael will see to it—but in a different way than would happen through humans."

"Always when a human being avoids work, the spiritual world is calling on him or her to accomplish it. When the Earth transitions into its Jupiter condition the task that was set for it in this period of evolution must be done. We want to unroll the great future picture that is present when the Earth is ripe for the Jupiter condition. Through the people who have genuinely worked it will, in part, be entirely spiritualized, and these people will live in a wonderful paradise."

"However, through the people who have let their organ dry up, part of the Earth will also be hardened, like a small kernel, so to speak, shrunk together, and the people who live on it will not perceive the others; the others will not be present for them. They will not be mature enough to enter the Jupiter condition and for this reason will be carried over in the womb of spiritual beings; and it will be shown to them one how difficult it is not to have kept pace with evolution. Humans have only had this Earth period to educate themselves to freedom and by means of it to love. And for this work we should obtain strength in our meditations. Sooner or later, indeed, through our meditation, we will get to know spiritual world that surround us. However, we should bear in mind that it should happen with the proper attitude; which we like to call inquisitiveness; but rather, in order to help humanity with progress to freedom and love."

Esoteric Lessons 1904-1909, **Rudolf Steiner, Notes from the collection of Elizabeth Vreede Stuttgart, August 9, 1908, GA 266/1**

"There are many people who think that they take pains for the salvation of humankind from morning to evening. But it is questionable whether this is in fact the case. Clairvoyant sight has shown that strivings for the salvation of humanity that come out of materialistic thinking do precisely what works wrongly. And it can lie in the karma of a person that he or she should not be active in this service but rather should wait until the time of maturity has arrived for a specific task. Then such a task can be gently whispered to him or her by higher beings and therefore not be caused by outer circumstances."

"During waking day life all kinds of sense impressions influence human beings. For those who are entirely devoted to the impressions of the outer world then determine what is taken up.

Because of this, in the night, the human astral body is confused and torn and cannot be put in order by spiritual beings. For such people life is then a process of destruction."

"Esotericists are distinguished through the fact that they mediate, immerse themselves in their own experience and thereby let their lives be determined less by external circumstances. Those who again and again strive in meditation are not exposed at night to the astral confusions and make themselves capable of receiving instruction from spiritual beings. And it is very necessary that we be instructed in this way. For since November 1879 we have entered into a new stage of human evolution. Then the Archangel Gabriel's leadership of humankind was concluded. Gabriel had worked for four hundred years on the formation of a new organ in the human brain by regulating and determining births. He is also the one who proclaimed the birth of the Savior to the Virgin Mary. (*Luke* 1:28-38) The new organ that thus only since Gabriel's regency, since the beginning of those four hundred years, is given to us, gives us the possibility of understanding spiritual truths. People in the sixteenth century would not have had any understanding for our theosophy. The successor of the Archangel Gabriel, the Archangel Michael, now has the responsibility for stimulating humans to use this newly acquired organ. Those who do not use it let it decay and fall into ruin. Such people then fall under the influence of Michael's adversary, Mammon or Beelzebub. He is the god of hindrances, who wants to hinder humankind from advancing. Under his influence bacteria and bacilli also come into existence. In this way, in the future, horrible epidemics could arise, also strange neurological disorders. Children would be born into the world with ruined nervous systems."

"After a further four hundred years Michael's leadership will be followed by that of the Archangel Oriphiel [2,229 AD], who also reigned at the time of Christ's birth [Archangelic Period of Oriphiel (200 BC-150 AD)]. Oriphiel gives divine wrath, but only those who have achieved a high level of development are allowed to express this wrath. Jesus also drove the moneychangers out of the temple." [*Matthew* 21:12; *Mark* 11:15; *John* 2:12]

The Biography of the Great I Am

Any attempt to describe the mysterious and ubiquitous 'I Am' (Ego) of the human being can only fail to do what all philosophy, epistemology, religion, myth, fable, parable, or moral story has tried to do before, and also failed—to define the human 'I', or 'I Am.' In fact, all architecture, literature, music, art, and culture has been an attempt to define the human 'I Am' and its relationship to the world, other human beings, and the divine. Existentially speaking, a conscious human being can only be so because of conceptualizations that arise from perception of the world and others. In other words, the development of the 'I Am.'

Through interaction with the world and others, humans can understand their personal 'I Am', as well as those of others. This reciprocal relationship of 'I and Thou' or 'I and the World' creates the knowledge that the human 'I Am' must have to objectively live and grow. The ultimate question about the difference between the Great (Godly) 'I Am' and the Small (Human) 'I Am' was answered by the ancient Hindus in their philosophical explanations found in their holy writings called the *Upanishads*. These books of wisdom indicate that the world—Brahman—and the objective, individual human 'I Am'—Atman—are essentially the same in nature and being. In other words, the ultimate and the relative, the general and the particular, the 'I Am' and the 'World' are actually one. The human being's 'I Am' and the Cosmos are the same—they are one—they are a 3D hologram of each other that continues to contribute to cosmic creation by adding human individualized replicas to the cosmic whole—the One Cosmos.

Essentially, through creation from nothingness, the gods made new gods. The human 'I Am' is a divine co-creator with the Divine, and thus is the 'answer to the question of the universe' and is, as John Dee claimed, the 'Hieroglyphic Monad.' The human 'I Am' bridges the gap between self and world, self and others, and self and God.

The evolving human being has taken on many forms throughout history and will take on many more in the future as we metamorphose alongside our solar system. Therefore, the human 'I Am' changes over time from a simple globe of warmth into a shining globe of warmth, light, sound, and life—just like our Sun does through its loving gifts to humanity and the Earth. The human body will ultimately transform into a glowing ball of transparent luminous carbon—a liquid diamond of sorts—similar to what most cosmic bodies become over time. The human replication of the cosmic 'nature and being' of God is evolving over time, and in the far future humanity will become a living Cosmos of Celestial Stars ('Zodiac'), when human development evolves into Angels, Archangels, Archai and beyond. Once humans become Archai Beings—Beings of Time—and evolve to the point of preparing to become Elohim, Spirits of Form, they will be able to help sustain their own individual 'Zodiac,' according to Rudolf Steiner. This Archai nature of the human 'I Am' will have to ascend in evolution into higher ranks of the spiritual hierarchies to take on those duties. For humans, space and time are seemingly insurmountable forces that cannot be overcome at this stage of development with the child-like consciousness that most human beings currently manifest. The angelic hosts are not subject to time, space, or limited consciousness.

The biography of the 'Cosmic I Am,' the 'Great I Am,' is interlocked with the evolving biography of humanity. The Cosmos (Universe) that humans believe they perceive and understand at this point in time, is directly tied to the level of consciousness of the observer. As humanity evolves, so does its understanding of everything outside of itself, including our solar system, our galaxy, the super-galaxy, and the Universe. As the Hermetic Emerald Tablet of the Egyptians tells us:

"That which is above is like to that which is below, and that which is below is like that which is above." The same is true for the macrocosm of our Universe and the microcosm of the human constitution. Over the entire time of humanity's creation and growth, the Small 'I Am' will become the image and likeness of the 'Great I Am.'

We can understand human spiritual evolution through the simple idea that the human being contains many worlds of bacteria, enzymes, DNA, blood corpuscles, nerves, that we can barely 'see', as well as trillions of interactions happening in the human body all at once in the metabolic system, and yet the human 'I Am' consciousness is barely aware of these worlds that constitute the major parts of its life and existence. When the human being looks out into the celestial sky and sees untold numbers of stars, galaxies, and trillions of interactions per second in the twinkling night sky, all beyond the scope of human consciousness, the hidden world of the microcosm in the human metabolic system can be seen standing at the other end of the spectrum from the macrocosmic starry sky. The human being stands in the middle between the realms below (metabolism) and above (starry heavens) with human consciousness that is blurred at either end of the spectrum. Throughout it all, the human being participates in a reciprocal symbiotic and loving relationship with that which is above and below. The human being truly is the universal hieroglyph, the holy grail of life, both in the macrocosmic Universe and in the microcosmic mysteries found in the human body.

Most of what we can discuss concerning the human 'I Am' comes from belief, faith, religion, myth, legend, tradition, revelation, and many other sources that would not please the modern secular humanist scientist who is limited to the five senses and what can be measured, weighed, and ascribed a number. You can look inside yourself and find many answers—like the Help Menu on a computer. Many people would say that the human is already complete and that the only Master the higher human self needs is already provided through the spiritual constitution of the human being. Each human being has their 'higher self,' 'higher I Am' that is a master being from the future who is ready to teach us what we can become, much like our Guardian Angel.

The aspirant can also choose the path of faith and create a Christian cosmology that provides answers to the most important questions of life: Who Am I; where did I come from; where am I now, and where am I going? Notice that all of these questions are about the existential question concerning the human 'I Am.' To study the 'I Am' we are, in fact, studying the nature and being of 'was', 'is' and 'will be,' the past, present, and future—the Alpha and Omega or the biography of the 'Great I Am.'

The questions about the nature of 'being' itself address the 'I Am' and its mission. From ancient history we hear this question being answered by Isis, the Queen of the Sun and Moon. In Egypt, at the Temple of Sais, is an inscription on a statue of Isis holding her son Horus that reads: "I am Isis, I am the past, the present, and the future. No man has lifted my veil and lived; the fruit that I bore was the Sun."

The inscription of Isis at Sais describing her nature and being gives humanity a key to what we all ca become in the future. Isis is another name for Sophia, or Wisdom of the Soul. Isis goes through an initiation to rise from the Earth to the Moon, and then to the Sun. Osiris, her husband, is killed by an evil brother, and Isis cannot put Osiris completely back together again and must ascend and assume his throne as she becomes the Queen of the Sun and Osiris descends to become King of the Underworld. Between the Earth and Sun, Isis gives birth to her Son, the Hawk-headed Horus, who becomes the Sun of the world in a greater fashion than either his Mother or Father. Thus, an image arises that Isis gives birth to her higher self, who is her son Horus. The solar myth becomes the transformation of Isis, Osiris, and Horus—Father, Mother and the Child who is greater than both. It is the same solar myth found in many ancient cultures and is a perfect analogy for the developing human spiritual nature. This is the same journey each human being must knowingly undertake on the spiritual path.

Each of the three deities (Isis, Osiris, Horus—Father, Mother, and the Son who is greater than both) is a living part of the aspirant when the 'I Am' directs the spiritual soul to unite with the higher Ego (Spirit-Self). In a way, we are Isis who can birth the Sun (Christ) of the higher self and take-up her throne again upon the Sun to help her Son rule the world. Isis can be imagined as the transformed Earth becoming a Sun, while Horus is the Sun of the Solar System—the 'Great I Am.' Isis/Sophia transforms Her creation while Christ, Her Son, transforms every ascending human being. The soul gives birth to the spirit, which ultimately becomes the selfless higher 'I Am,' and unites with the 'Great I Am.' Whether physically through ancient myths, or cosmically through Christian cosmology, the 'I Am' births the spirit that yearns to re-unite with the 'Great I Am'—Christ.

The propensity to find the solar hero exists in almost every pre-Christian mythology, religion, tradition, and legend. There are authors like Kersey Graves, who in his book, *The World's Sixteen Crucified Saviors*, tries to make the case that because there were many pre-Christian crucified gods, solar heroes, sun gods, harvest gods, and other traditions that naively believed in the 'Sun saving humanity,' that Jesus Christ was just another silly superstition following in the footsteps of sixteen previous solar gods. It is interesting to note that this tradition was ancient and ubiquitously found throughout the whole world. Robert Graves, often citing *Anacalypsis* and other works by Godfrey Higgins (1772–1833) as his source, asserts that many messiah-like saviors were crucified on a cross or tree before ascending into heaven. Many other forms of death also were used on a variety of cultural heroines and heroes to aid in the process of their death and resurrection. Here is the short list of Robert Graves' examples of pre-Christian Crucified Saviors:

> Thalis of Egypt (1700 BC), Krishna of India, (1200 BC), Crite of Chaldea, (1200 BC), Atys of Phrygia, (1170 BC), Tammuz of Syria (1160 BC), Hesus or Eros (834 BC), Bali of Orissa (725

BC), Indra of Tibet (725 BC), Iao of Nepal (622 BC), Mithra of Persia (600 BC), Alcestos of Euripides (600 BC), Quezalcoatl of Mexico (587 BC), Wittoba of the Bilingonese (552 BC), Prometheus (547 BC), Quirinus of Rome (506 BC).

As you can see by the list, some of these beings are well known and certainly do seem to follow an ancient tradition. But this list is much too short to demonstrate that this long-lasting tradition had many names besides just Crucified Saviors. There are also other solar heroes and heroines who come to mind when thinking back through mythology and religion. Solar deities are often referred to as 'the dying and rising deity.' These beings are found in most ancient religions, myths, and beliefs. Some of them are well known to Westerners while others are more obscure. A short list of these Solar Deities who die and resurrect are:

Osiris, Tammuz, Adonis, Attis, Dionysus, Baldur, Quetzalcoatl, Izanami, Ishtar, Persephone, Psyche, Osiris, Heracles, Hermes, Aeneas, Orpheus, Alcestis, Theseus, Hippolyta, Sisyphus, Odysseus, Yama, Yima, Dumuzi, Tammuz, Innana, Baldur, Ishtar, Persephone, Psyche, and Aeneas.

Harvest Gods and Solar Heroes

Below we present a partial list of a number of other historical characters who came from heaven and took on human form, died, and then ascended back into heaven. This follows the pattern of Harvest Gods who remain alive if the harvest is good but must be sacrificed if the harvest is bad so they might return to heaven as an offering for a better harvest next year. They were sometimes referred to as Wicker Kings. In ancient Celtic culture, it was often the case that the king was king as long as the harvest was good. Otherwise, the first male child born after the Winter Solstice was chosen to be the 'king for the year' and would be burnt alive as a human sacrifice if he had not brought

Harvest Gods and Solar Heroes

on a good harvest. Only if the harvest was good could the king live for another year. The Wicker King's fate was directly tied to the gifts of the Sun and its bounty.

The Harvest King is a type of savior tied to the annual forces of nature. Often, pagan crucified saviors accomplished heroic feats to save the tribe from disaster or perhaps they simply descended into the underworld for some purpose or another and then returned to life on Earth demonstrating that they had 'conquered death.' Either way, they faced death and returned a hero of the Sun. This pattern is, of course, an animistic practice that believed the Earth dies each year and must be born again in the Spring. It is like the ancient Greeks who believed that the Sun god drove the chariot across the sky in the daytime and descended into the underworld at night. In those days, only a hero with awakened mystery wisdom would know otherwise.

Here is a list of the few heroes who die and come back to life in one manner or another including the classic descent into hell or the underworld:

> Heracles of Greece, Salivahana of Bermuda, Osiris of Egypt, Oru of Egypt, Zoroaster of Persia, Baal of Phoenicia, Taut "the Only BEgotten of God" of Phoenicia, Bali of Afghanistan, Zalmoxis of Thrace, Zoar of the Bonzes, Adad of Assyria, Deva Tat of Siam of Thailand, Sammonocadam of Siam, Alcides of Thebes, Mikado of the Sintoos, Beddru of Japan, Bremrillah of the Druids, Cadmus of Greece, Gentaut of Mexico, Fohi of China, Tien of China, and Ixion of Rome.

It has often been conjectured that the details of Jesus Christ's birth, life, death, resurrection, and ascension are not original but are shared with multiple other gods or deities of older religions. For example, the god Horus, an Egyptian God representing the Sun, worshiped around 3000 BC., has the following list of defining characteristics—which just happen to be similar to a list we could make of Jesus of Nazareth.

1. Born on December 25th
2. Born of a virgin
3. Birth was accompanied by a star in the east
4. After his birth he was adored by three kings
5. Teacher at age 12
6. Baptized and ministry began at age 30
7. Had twelve disciples he traveled with
8. Performed miracles: healing the sick, walking on water, etc.
9. Names: Lamb of God, The Truth, The Light, The Good Shepard, The Way, etc.
10. Betrayed by a desciple
11. Crucified on a tree or cross
12. Dead for three days
13. Resurrected and ascended into the spiritual world

Some of these attributes are also shared by other gods in different cultures over time:

- Attis (Greece, 1200 BC)—Attributes 1, 2, 11, 12, 13
- Krishna (India, 900 BC)—Attributes 2, 3, 8, 13
- Dionysos (Greece, 500 BC)—Attributes 1, 2, 8, 9, 13, plus turning water into wine (a.k.a. God's Son, Alpha and Omega)
- Mithras (Persia, 1200 BC)—Attributes 1, 2, 7, 8, 12, 13, 9, (a.k.a. The Truth, The Light)

Christ has Always Been Present

Although Christ appeared only later, He was always present in the spiritual sphere of the Earth. Already in the ancient Oracles of Atlantis, the priests of those Oracles spoke of the 'Spirit of the Sun,' of Christ. In the ancient Indian age of civilization, the Holy Rishis spoke of Vishva Karman; Zarathustra in ancient Persia spoke of Ahura Mazdao; Hermes of Osiris, and Moses spoke of the power which, being eternal, brings about the harmonization of the temporal and natural, the power living in the Ehjeh asher Ehjeh ('I am that I Am'), the harbinger of Christ.

Ancient traditions and mystery schools spoke of the coming of Christ, the solar hero (word or logos) from the Sun. But where was Christ to be found in those ancient times? He was found in the realm to which the eye of spirit alone can penetrate; He was found in the spiritual world on the Sun in the Mother Lodge of Humanity. It is Christ, working from the realm of the Sun even before humanity appeared on Earth, who created the possibility of human life and mitigated humanity's negative karma through His Pre-Earthly Deeds. Then, Christ came in a human body to the Earth (only once) through His Fourth Deed—the Mystery of Golgotha -; and since then the physical Earth and human physical bodies have been transformed and re-enlivened.

Rudolf Steiner spoke about what Christ accomplished in the Earthly sphere before His incarnation and the significance of the Mystery of Golgotha and its effects upon those who at that time were in the spiritual world between physical incarnations. We are also told that on Golgotha, when Christ's blood flowed from His wounds, Christ appeared in the underworld flooding it with light and redeeming the faithful. The appearance of Christ on the Earth is an event of supreme importance, but it is also highly significant for the realms through which humanity passes between death and a new birth. Christ is now the Guardian of the Threshold and the Lord of Karma and His influence is unparalleled in all spiritual and physical realms.

The biography of the 'Great I Am' is the biography of Christ, the Second Person in the Holy Trinity who worked through the seven leading Elohim to create the form of the human 'I Am.' Christ's nature as either 'begotten' (birthed) or already pre-existent to creation as a 'co-creator' with the Father God is debated by many theologians. We know from Steiner's indications that Christ created the human 'I Am' (Ego) through the Seven Elohim and placed it in the soul of each human being; and now, like the Hindu god Vishnu, is the sustainer and maintainer of the divine plan of the Cosmos to help humans evolve into Angels. Christ was the Group-soul of all humans to begin with; but Christ wishes for His creation to become co-creators with the Holy Trinity and the spiritual hierarchy.

When the original Adam soul was created, a twin soul called Adam Kadmon was also created that did not descend with Adam to the Garden of Eden. Adam's twin 'sister soul' remained perfect and under the care of Christ in the Sun Mother Lodge of Humanity, near the throne of God. In fact, all human souls have a twin sister soul that has been kept safe in the spiritual world, in the Sun Temple. Humans on Earth only have access to their lower 'I Am' or earthly Ego. This earthly Ego comes to birth through interacting with the world and other beings. Once the earthly Ego develops through the Sentient Soul, Intellectual Soul, and Consciousness Soul realms, the elements of universal wisdom build the human being's three higher Egos in the realms of Spirit-Land. After advancing much further in the future, humans will eventually embody three realms of the spiritual world (Spirit-Self, Life-Spirit, Spirit Human) where all three 'higher Egos' are waiting to incorporate into the spiritual constitution of the human being that will subsequently develop into higher Angelic hierarchies.

Adam Kadmon

Throughout creation, Christ battles with Lucifer and Ahriman who have attempted to destroy the Divine Plan by introducing challenges to humans that cause many to stubble and fall. Lucifer and Ahriman both 'fell' from heaven and have tried to bring humanity down with them into the lower sub-natural realms of evil and darkness. To prevent a total subversion of human evolution by these adversarial powers, the spiritual world intervened to hold back and protect a portion of the original Adam soul, called Adam Kadmon. Lucifer's original attack was upon Adam's astral body of desires, while a portion of Adam's etheric body was protected and held back in the spiritual world as a pure and undefiled part of Adam's nature. This was done by Christ to prevent Adam's etheric body from being infected by Lucifer. Various spiritual traditions and mythological accounts describe this preservation and protection of the pure Adam soul, Adam Kadmon. Certainly, the *Genesis* account of the Tree of Knowledge of Good and Evil and the Tree of Life can be seen as a living imagination of these events.

In the *Genesis* story, during the time of the temptation, Adam and Eve were given access to the Tree of Knowledge of Good and Evil, but the Tree of Life was held back from them and access was denied. Similarly, a portion of the etheric body of Adam was held back in the spiritual world, protected from the evil temptations of Lucifer and Ahriman. This pure Adam, Adam Kadmon, was actively involved in human development. From the beginning of human evolution on Earth, Adam Kadmon was open and receptive to being a helper of Christ who intervened in human evolution on behalf of Christ. Long before the actual incarnation of Christ in Jesus of Nazareth, Adam Kadmon and Christ worked together to enable the human being to maintain and develop its uniquely human nature, in spite of the attacks of evil adversarial spirits. These crucial turning points of human spiritual evolution were performed by Christ working through Adam Kadmon to assure the Divine Plan could be carried out, and that Christ and the good spirits prevail.

Early in the Lemurian Epoch, Lucifer and Ahriman continued their onslaught against the human being and caused a disruption of the human senses. This attack on the senses brought humanity under the influence of Earth forces that threatened to pull the human being downward and keep humanity in the horizontal posture of animals. Christ joined with Adam Kadmon, who assumed the form of an Archai, and balanced the human senses giving humanity the capacity to rise-up from the predominately horizontal posture and stand upright, freeing the arms and hands for human deeds distinct from animals. Only as an erect, upright being could humans receive the uniquely human 'I Am' (Ego) as a gift from Christ and the Spirits of Form (Elohim). This First Pre-Earthly Deed of Christ advanced the human soul and created the ground into which the human Ego could be planted. This First Pre-Earthly Deed of Christ and Adam Kadmon, the ability to stand upright, is recapitulated in the development of a young child who raises herself from the horizontal posture and learns to stand upright and walk.

This was not, however, the end of this primordial luciferic and ahrimanic onslaught, and in the middle of the Atlantean Epoch these adversaries strove to disrupt the proper functioning of the human vital organs. Their effort was to render the human vital organs incapable of relating correctly with the outside world, to make these organs, in Steiner's vivid term, 'selfish.' The result was that with the turning inward of the human organs, human speech was threatened with becoming purely subjective, capable of only subjective, animal-like emotional outbursts—cries of pain, joy, meaningless babbling.

Again, the Christ-permeated Adam Kadmon, acting now through the realm of the Archangels, intervened to reorder the organs and give to human speech the possibility to express objective reality. By the end of the Atlantean Epoch, however, Lucifer and Ahriman were continuing their attack on the human being by disrupting and disordering the basic human soul functions of thinking, feeling, and willing. This disorder was reflected again in a threat to human speech, that it would never be able to grasp and express meaning. Once again, the Christ-permeated Adam Kadmon intervened to reorder human speech so that it could be uniquely human, that is, that it would be capable of grasping and expressing meaning—meaning in the world and meaning in the human soul. This balancing of human speech through Christ and the Adam

Kadmon was the Second Pre-Earthly Deed of Christ which He accomplished long before He came to the Earth.

Rudolf Steiner once commented that today a child learns to speak but can do so only because of these last two deeds of Christ—the one to give to human speech the capacity to be objective and the other to give the capacity to grasp and express meaning. Rudolf Steiner said: "We can enrich anew our inner feelings if we remember that when we see a child beginning to speak and gradually improving his power of expression, that the Christ-impulse rules within the unconscious nature and that the Christ-force lives in the child's power of speech, guarding and stimulating it."

The Third Pre-Earthly Deed of Christ and Adam Kadmon was to bestow upon humans the ability to think clear thoughts and to be able to objectify the outer world into concepts and to perceive inwardly the mental images created through perception. Once again, Lucifer and Ahriman tried to ruin the properly timed gifts of the spirit by giving an over-abundance of ungrounded thinking to the human being on Atlantis, or to draw down the gifts of thinking into sub-natural realms of evil that extinguish the light of human thinking. Christ's third deed prepared the way for humans to be free thinking beings who could then accept the most important gift of self-conscious awareness of the human 'I Am' and its destiny to evolve into an Angel.

The Fourth Deed of Christ was a tremendous deed of sacrifice that brought the 'I Am' of the human being to its next step of spiritual evolution. The Incarnation of Christ into a physical body, and the ensuing Mystery of Golgotha, was the Turning Point of Time and was the most important deed of human history. This Fourth Deed of Christ, involving once more a union of the Christ and Adam Kadmon, was the redemption of the human 'I Am' and the redemption of the dying Earth. Other great masters and avatars were also involved in this Fourth Deed. Even the Persian Priest-King Zarathustra and Gautama Buddha were involved in this momentous deed. Zarathustra was one of the two Jesus children whose birth in Jerusalem was described the *Gospel of Matthew*. Adam Kadmon was incarnated in the Essene community in Nazareth as the other Jesus child. This child was born to a similarly pure being like Adam Kadmon, Mary of Nazareth. There were two Marys and two Jesus children. These mysteries of Jesus Christ, and Mary Sophia are the deepest secrets and mysteries of human evolution. Reading Steiner's *Fifth Gospel* provides the aspirant with a view of these mysteries that is found nowhere else.

One might call the Second Coming of Christ in the Etheric the Fifth Deed of Christ that once again defended the human soul from Lucifer and Ahriman. Christ came into a physical body once, and only once, through Jesus of Nazareth, and now manifests in His etheric body in the super-etheric realm around the Earth, Shambhala. Christ's appearance in the etheric is the second most important event in human history, according to Dr. Steiner. The entire evolution of human development could be derailed if Christ is crucified in the etheric by Ahriman's materialistic hold on humanity. This Fifth Deed is the salvation of life on Earth and life in the human etheric body just as the Fourth Deed was the salvation of the physical realm of Earth and the human physical body.

In the distant future, Steiner tells us that there will be a Sixth and Seventh Deed of Christ which will redeem the astral realm and the realm of the Ego, the Christened 'I Am.' After these two future Deeds of Christ, He will have redeemed the physical, etheric, astral, and Ego realms of the Earth and the human constitution. Christ will also be involved in the ascension of human beings into the realms of their three higher Egos, Spirit-Self, Life-Spirit, and Spirit Human.

Another deed of Christ was to create and sustain human memory. This deed happened as a result of Christ's redemption of the etheric realms where memory lives and is stored. To these deeds we must also add the visit of Christ when He spoke to Arjuna through his charioteer in the voice of Krishna. This conversation is recorded in the *Bhagavad Gita* and constitutes Christ's instructions to humanity as it was entering the Kali Yuga, the age of darkness. The deeds of Christ were necessary for the evolution of humanity to continue in a healthy fashion and to counteract the attacks of Lucifer and Ahriman. Much like Vishnu the sustainer god, who maintained the creation of Brahma, Christ similarly helps create the Father God's kingdoms and sustains the human 'I Am' throughout all time. Christ also sacrificed Himself, with the help of Adam Kadmon, to sustain the 'I Am' as it develops utilizing the Deeds of Christ to inherent the gifts of uprightness, speech, thinking, birth the free 'I Am', and the development of human memory that can be carried from life to life. These Deeds of Christ made it possible for the influence of Lucifer and Ahriman to be counterbalanced and redeemed. Without these deeds, the 'Small I Am' has no chance to grow into the 'Great I Am.'

Rudolf Steiner tells us that Krishna was directly connected to Christ's deeds and that his mission was to educate humanity about the nature of the human Ego before Christ's Deed of birthing a conscious Ego in every human being. One can only imagine that Steiner is indicating, as he did with Buddha, that Christ is the great teacher of the gods and deities also.

It is possible to see the ten incarnations of Vishnu, as sustainer of humanity, as the ten months a child spends in the womb of its mother. Each incarnation of Vishnu has been compared to a monthly stage of human development in utero. Is it possible that Vishnu is another name for the pre-Christian workings of the Cosmic Christ who obviously tends the human child carefully from birth to age 21 when Ego development begins properly? Christ is the sustainer and the creator of the Ego; therefore, the work of sustaining the developing embryo is yet another deed of Christ.

Associating Christ with Krishna/Vishnu makes sense in the overall development of the 'I Am' (Ego). Likewise, it makes perfectly good sense that Christ is also the midwife of the physical body just as He and the Adam Kadmon are the midwives of standing, speaking, thinking, and memory.

The Pre-Earthly Deeds of Christ are exclusively elaborated upon by Rudolf Steiner and stand as one of the most incredible insights about the nature of the Cosmic Christ that can be found in any Christian cosmology. These profound insights are only equaled by Dr. Steiner's gift of *The Fifth Gospel* which illuminates the missing years of Jesus of Nazareth and the mystery wisdom of the Cosmic Christ found in the *Gospels*. With these insights we can begin to fill in many of the missing pieces to the biography of the 'Great I Am' and its child the 'Small I Am.'

Christ's Influence on Human Development

As the educational process of Rudolf Steiner strives to address itself to the principle of the higher nature of man, the Christ-principle, upon which all of Anthroposophy is built; it has at its source the wellspring of ever inspirational material which cosmogenically and anthropogenically associate man with his hierarchical nature as a spiritual being. We can find the pure picture of this hierarchical relationship in the child's development. Christ's revelation is found in every young child. Christ's presence resurrects the etheric body of the Earth, and man can demonstrate this characteristic renewal in his own selfless behavior. This can be seen clearly in the innocence and purity of a handicapped child or in the newborn baby, up to the age of three. Very young children are still embraced in the Christened etheric envelope of the Earth which maintains its upbuilding forces ever anew. A child can, throughout its life, demonstrate this inherited source of strength. This source is the 'Great I Am' which germinates the seeds of wisdom and love in individual consciousness giving it the strength and motivation to evolve.

In the first three years of the child, some of the greatest tasks of its life are performed with incredible powers against odds seemingly insurmountable. The strength of will, perseverance, balance, and skill are paramount in the child who learns to roll over, crawl, pull-up, stand, and balance himself on his/her own two feet. It is through the power of imitation that this process of balance is observed, learned, and developed. The striving 'to be' and 'to imitate' is unquenchable in the waking life of a child this age. The temperamental differentiations are myriad, but the single direction and outcome can be seen. Learning to move about and develop the arms, legs, torso, and speech organs of throat, lung, and brain into complex forms of woven patterns with minute differentiations and multi-leveled meanings and ramifications is almost incomprehensible to the rational mind. But the Christened soul is beyond the rational mind, and the Ego of a young child must go through tremendous challenges to become conscious. The child must establish, separate, recognize, and reflect upon the nature of his or her own individuality and its subjective relationship to the world of nature.

Observations of these events go beyond any explanations in the fields of philosophy, science, psychology, or education. The three processes of standing erect and walking, speaking, and thinking are the most mysterious, wondrous, and misunderstood processes in human development. There is much work and good effort done by psychologists in observation, examination, calculation, and experimentation; but there are no comprehensive theories that explain these mysteries. In the end, all stand in confused consternation at the abilities of the natural, healthy child growing in its environment.

In Spiritual Science, Dr. Steiner has pointed the way for deeper inner work in meditation on the unfoldment of the gifts of childhood. Out of active work and communion with these forces can we come to behold and understand what is meant by the following picture given by Dr. Steiner in the lecture series entitled *The Spiritual Guidance of Man* (The Anthroposophic Press, Spring Valley, N.Y., 1950, p.17-18):

> "It was the deeds of the Christ which intervened and built the possibility of human Ego development through three specific Pre-Earthly Deeds and the culmination of creation in the

Fourth Deed called the Mystery of Golgotha. The First Deed was accomplished during the Lemurian times in what has been subsequently called The Garden of Eden."

The First Deed of Christ accomplished the gift of man's upright posture and subsequently the ability to walk. Secondly, in the Atlantean times there was a type of 'Garden of Eden'; and there too, Christ's Second Deed accomplished the selfless ordering of humanity's sense organs; or simply stated, the gift of speech in man. Later, in Atlantean times, the Third Deed selflessly ordered man's vital organs into a cooperative thinking, feeling, and willing. In the Atlantis Epoch, when the human being faced a distortion of the seven vital organs from the adversarial powers that would have made our organs selfishly fight against each other, there was a need for the Second Pre-Earthly Deed of Christ. Working in the realm of the Elohim with Adam Kadmon [Nathan Soul], Christ sacrificed his etheric forces so that human language could be objective—able to channel creatively the 'Word' of God in truth.

These Pre-Earthly Deeds of Christ are cosmic in origin and should be presented in Rudolf Steiner's own words from: *Background to the Mystery of Golgotha*, Rudolf Steiner, Lecture VII, *The Pre-Earthly Deeds of Christ*, Pforzheim, March 7, 1914, GA 152:

> "It is this upright position that the child learns to acquire before the awakening of his Ego's consciousness. In our present Post-Atlantean life, we recapitulate those things which, as man, we have acquired only in the course of the ages. This power to stand and to walk in an upright position was acquired by slow stages in the old Lemurian Epoch, and we now recapitulate it in infancy before our Ego awakens to consciousness. This pre-knowledge is crowded into a time of life when the process does not yet depend upon our consciousness but works as an unconscious-impulse towards the upright position."

"...this came about because, during the Earth development, the Spirits of Form poured the Ego into man out of their own substance. And the first manifestation of this inflowing of the 'I' was that inner force by means of which man raised himself into an upright position."

"...the Atlantean man was actually the first to learn to speak, and the Akashic Records show how that came about. Learning to speak is the second capacity which a child acquires before the actual Ego-consciousness awakens, the awakening coming after he has learnt to speak. Learning to speak depends altogether on a kind of imitation; the aptitude for which, however, is deeply imbedded in human nature. Speech creates a consequence of progressive development. The Spirits of Form poured themselves into man and created him, and thereby he became able to speak a language, to live his earth life on the physical plane."

"...through the fact that for the second time the Being in the etheric heights, who later became the Nathan-Jesus [Adam Kadmon] child, received into himself the Christ-being who henceforward permeated the bodily organs of man; man became capable of uttering more than interjections. The power of grasping the objective was brought about through the Second Christ-event [Pre-Earthly Deed]."

"...then came the Third Christ-event [Pre-Earthly Deed]. For the third time that Being in the spiritual heights, later to be born as the Nathan-Jesus, united himself with the Christ-Being and again poured the forces received into the human power of speech. In this way it was made possible for the power of speech to create, by means of words, actual signs representative of the external environment, thus enabling mankind to create language as a means of communication between the different inhabited regions."

"...in order that thinking too might be united with the Christ-impulse, that thinking as such might not come into disorder in its activity on the Ego; there came the Fourth Christ-event [Deed], the Mystery of Golgotha."

These deeds of Christ are of a cosmic and historic origin. Christ is a being whose destiny is interlocked with the destiny of humanity. Before the beginning of time, Christ was, and He had planned that man would come forth out of the sacrifice of the spiritual hierarchies. We belong as much to that world of spirit in our sleep as we do to the world around us in our waking life. Let us hear what Dr. Steiner has to say about this relationship in his lecture cycle entitled, *Education as a Social Problem,* Rudolf Steiner, Lecture I, *Historical Requirements of the Present Time, Dornach,* August 9, 1919, GA 296:

"When a child enters the physical existence, she only continues the experience she had in the world prior to conception. There we live as human beings, within the beings of the higher hierarchies; we do what originates as impulses from the nature of the higher hierarchies. There we are imitators to a much higher degree because we are united with the beings we imitate. Then we are placed into the physical world. In it we continue our habit of being one with our surroundings. This habit then extends to being one with our surroundings. This habit then extends to being one with and imitating the people around us who have to take care of a child's education by doing, thinking, and feeling only what he may imitate. The benefit for a child is all the greater the more he is able to live not in his own soul but in those within his environment."

As a human being comes forth as an infant to face the world, there is a whole evolutionary history of mankind that he must catch up to in his development. The previous development of human attainments must be met fresh by the newly developing child. These tasks, or personal orientations to his own self and others, are a matter of imitative behavior structuring or modeling. To orient, communicate, and understand others of your kind; one must merge with the mannerisms and examples of his/her caretakers. Behavior is partly the accumulated experience of all members of your species. This pool of evolutionary strivings and attainments becomes the nourishment of the newborn who drinks in his surroundings deeply.

Each new citizen of the human race recapitulates the past development of the whole species. The deeds of ancient Lemuria, Atlantis, and the Post-Atlantean Epoch are lived again microcosmically within the individual. Once again, the Pre-Earthly and Earthly Deeds of Christ in history become apparent before the watchful eye. The importance of this first period of life for a child is heard in these words by Rudolf Steiner from the lecture cycle entitled *Soul Economy: Body, Soul and Spirit in Waldorf Education,* Rudolf Steiner, Lecture VII, *Children before the Seventh Year,* Stuttgart, December 29, 19121, GA 302:

> "The first two-and-a-half years are the most important of all; during this time the child is learning to walk and speak, and the formative forces of the head are shaping those organs which have the most intimate connection with the development and self-confidence of the individual in later life. In these years the child does really do everything of its own accord. It repels any will that seeks to impose itself from without. It works at the organization of its head with these forces which it has brought with it from a prenatal existence."

The child draws heavily upon its environment in these first years. Everything around the child including objects, feelings, sounds, thoughts, and spoken words penetrate right into the human organism and become the building material of the child's organs and bodily systems. The child absorbs through imitation all that is near it. Modern science has demonstrated this and named the ability of the body to resonate or imitate any spoken word, 'entrainment.' The child performs minute gestural body movements in repeatable patterns, even when it does not understand language yet. This is in keeping with Steiner's statement found in the lecture cycle, *Human Values in Education*, Rudolf Steiner, Lecture III, *Stages of Childhood*, Arnheim, July 19, 1924, GA 310:

> "While the human being is growing into the physical, earthly world, his inner nature is developing in such a way that this development proceeds in the first place out of gesture, out of differentiation of movement. The inner nature of the organism of speech develops out of movement in all its aspects and thought develops out of speech. This deeply significant law underlies all human development. Everything which makes its appearance in sound, in speech, is the result of gesture, mediated through the inner nature of the human organs..."

> "...Through his physical body the child is given over to everything in the nature of gesture; he cannot do otherwise than yield himself up to it. What we do later with our soul, and still later with our spirit, in that we yield ourselves up to the divine, even to the external world, as again spiritualized, this the child does with his physical body when he brings it into movement. He is completely immersed in religion, both with his good and his bad qualities. What remains with us as soul and spirit in later life, this the child has also in his physical organism."

This reaction in gesture to the spoken word is a great mystery that is intimately connected with the balance of the vital organs through the planetary influences which were brought under control by Christ through his Second Pre-Earthly Deed. The redemption of speech through harmonious breathing and circulation is a key to this mystery.

The First Pre-Earthly Deed of Christ, which attained man's upright position, made clear the possibility for speech to arise. If man were not upright, then speech could not occur. This orientation against gravity in alignment with the Cosmos is a truly solar principle of levity that places humanity midway between Heaven and Earth. This deed of uprightness was, of course, the First Pre-Earthly Deed of Christ. Its primacy was essential for the foundation of a speaking, thinking individual Ego.

Christ's Third Pre-Earthly Deed was the balancing of thinking, feeling, and willing which macrocosmically aligns Him with the Sun, Moon, and the Earth. This balance between these three cosmic forces also creates the harmonizing of the three soul powers of humanity. To stand erect means that the child attains the equilibrium of its own organism within the Cosmos and learns to control its movements while acquiring free orientation. Rudolf Steiner speaks of this in the following way from in a lecture from, *Waking, Speaking, Thinking—Imitation in a Bodily Religious Way,* April 15 to 22, 1923:

> "...the liberation of the hands and arms affords the possibility for the soul to find its equilibrium."

> "...the relation between physical equilibrium (action of the legs) and psychical equilibrium (action of the hands and arms) forms the foundation which enables the child to come into contact with the outer world through the medium of language."

> "...speech arises from the human being as a whole. The outer, rhythmical element arises from the movement of the legs, the inner thematic element from that of the hands and arms."

"...the child can only learn to think through learning to talk. Thinking can only arise out of speech and not before.

"...up to age seven the child imitates all that goes on in its surroundings in a bodily-religious way."

We can see by these statements made by Rudolf Steiner that the ability to think springs from speech and speech from the erect posture and all three from the balance of the forces of levity and gravity. This is simple, yet profound. But the three Pre-Earthly Deeds of Christ did not end there but reached its powerful shaping forces of form into the life of humanity again in the Post-Atlantean Period. Just when humanity's thinking had reached the lowest ebb and darkness had come upon the ancient clairvoyance so that truth was no longer self-evident, again Christ intervened to prevent humanity from losing the moral intention of thought.

The Mystery of Golgotha redeemed humanity's thoughts and instilled truth into the reality of thinking. Christ's death enlivened humanity's thoughts. Once again, a turning point and a strong gift of sacrifice was given to humanity by Christ. Christ's Deeds are not only of the past, but they lead also to a brighter future. Christ's mysteries are ever present and continuously unfolding. Rudolf Steiner tells us that new mysteries are to become known in the near future in the lecture: *Background of the Mystery of Golgotha*, Rudolf Steiner, Lecture VII, *Pre-Earthly Deeds of Christ*, Pforzheim, March 7, 1914, GA 152:

"For in addition to walking and standing upright, as well as speaking and thinking, the Christ-Force is now entering the memory. We can understand the Christ when He speaks to us through the Gospels. But we are only now being prepared as human beings for His entrance also into the thoughts which live in us and which then as remembered thoughts and ideas, live on further in us. And a time will come for humanity which is now being prepared but which will only be fulfilled in the

Sixth Great Period of humanity when men will look back upon that which they have lived through and experienced, upon that which lives on within them as memory. They will be able to realize that Christ Himself is present in the power of memory. He will be able to speak through every idea. And if we make concepts and ideas alive within us Christ will be united with our memories, with that which as our memory is so closely and intimately bound up with us."

For the gift of memory shall also be redeemed by Christ as another gift to mankind. As yet, only a sampling of Christ's true etheric form is manifesting to those who are in great need. But humanity shall benefit in a dramatic way from the gifts of the Lord of Karma, the Keeper of the Book of Life. The past, which is so intimately connected to the Deeds of Christ, shall open before us as the unveiled Akasha Records shall become the living memory of all His people.

It is instructive to examine a mantric verse which Rudolf Steiner gave to direct our attention to these powerful realities in: *Background of the Mystery of Golgotha*, Rudolf Steiner, Lecture VII *Pre-Earthly Deeds of Christ*, Pforzheim, March 7, 1914, GA 152:

"In the Primal Beginning was the power of Memory.
The power of Memory shall become Divine;
And a Divinity shall the power of Memory become.
All that arises within the Ego shall become
Something which has arisen out of the Christ-permeated,
God-permeated Memory.
In it shall be the Life,
In it shall be the radiant Light which,
Out of the Thinking which remembers,
Shines into the Darkness of the present time.
May that Darkness as it is today
Comprehend the Light of the Memory
Which has become Divine!"

These indications can bring you to surmise that the duties of a teacher take on a religious, reverential, devotional character. The following injunction of Rudolf Steiner's is a powerful revelation concerning the nature of a teacher: *The Essentials of Education*, Rudolf Steiner, Lecture II. Stuttgart April 9, 1924, GA 308:

> "...but whereas the child, with its physical body, develops into the religious mood of the believer, the teacher, inasmuch as he gazes at the wonders that are going on between birth and the change of teeth, develops into the religious attitude of the priest. The office of teacher becomes a priestly office, a kind of ritual performed at the altar of universal human life, not with the sacrificial offering that is to be led to death, but with the offering of human nature itself that is to be awakened to life."

The 'I Am' and Thou through Education

In the oldest writings of Humanity, we find a great dilemma. The *Upanishads* state that there are two things for man to know; first is the Atman, or that which is in man, and the second is Brahman, or that which is outside of man. The dilemma is that the Atman and Brahman are the same Being. Rudolf Steiner refers to the same dilemma in The *Philosophy of Spiritual Activity* when he states that all religion, art, and science come from the desire of man to bridge the gap between his 'I Am', or Self/Ego, and the world. Even though the names are different, the principle is the same.

Clearly, the resolution of conflict between the inner person and the outer world is an old and great task and it is this task that is the central theme of Rudolf Steiner's indications concerning Waldorf education. In Steiner's terms, this task can be stated as the development of a pedagogical atmosphere that engenders a wholesome relationship between the 'I Am', or Ego, of the child and the world.

The awakening of this I/Ego in a child can be seen in an especially pronounced fashion at the ages of three, nine, and eighteen years of age. At three, we often find that children are eager to attempt deeds in which they assert their Ego-hood. "I can do it myself," is a phrase quite common for this age child. While the three-year-old child's parent might refer to this stage of fanciful and aggressive tendencies as 'the terrible threes,' a Waldorf teacher sees these inclinations as the child's eagerness to attempt deeds through which she can assert her Ego-hood. This phase of development can be seen positively as the dawn of memory in the child's etheric body (life body), when events begin to impress themselves upon the astral body (desire body) which is the first sign of the development of a sense of Ego-hood. At the age of nine years, four months; we often find that children have a powerful experience as they begin to realize that their 'I Am' is bound and limited by their physical body. Before this revelation, the 'I Am' finds its home more in the head, the human representation of the starry heavens. The 'nine-year change,' as Rudolf Steiner called it, has now been documented by recent brain theories. It seems that the corpus callosum, which connects the right and left sides of the brain, doesn't finish its development until after nine years of age. Some brains studied didn't finish this development until age twelve, or in rare cases even as late as age fifteen. The child is used to right-brain activity of a kinesthetic, spatial, geometric, holistic, or full-bodied experience. As the corpus callosum finishes growing, left-brain activity becomes easier and going back and forth to right-brain/left-brain activities is accompanied by developing neurological capacities.

At this nine-year change, the I/Ego begins to descend from the head into the rhythmic system centered in the chest and then later even further into the metabolic processes (digestion, limb movement). It becomes more agitated as it meets the strong regular, rhythmic impulses of the heart and lung systems and subsequently the sense of oneness the child had until that time quickly disappears. The child becomes more controlled by strong, new emotions. Time and space, once integrated in the child's consciousness, become separated in a linear fashion, causing her direct experience of archetypal form to dissipate. She feels as if she is an orphan and asks tough questions about who she is and her limits. Talk of death, killing, and running away from home are common. It is at this point, when self-consciousness develops, that the child's need for music becomes paramount. Music provides harmony for these unsettled feelings. The various forms of music—singing, rhythmic movement, and poetry—are used to enhance main lesson teaching blocks in which the teacher holistically represents the world through the kingdoms of nature, beginning with animals, then plants, stones, and, finally, humanity itself.

At age eighteen, another Ego awareness experience usually manifests itself. The child becomes aware of her 'I Am' in the stream of life, and out of this sense, becomes aware of the need to direct her life's ambitions. Choosing vocations and other major decisions are a direct result of this eighteen-year-old Ego consciousness transition. What we as teachers must remember at this stage in the child's development is that she is becoming extremely critical of the authority of parents and other adults. Since we can teach little to an unwilling or rebellious child, we must always be aware that what we are, not only as teachers but also as human beings, stands clearly before the child and is part of the world from which her Ego develops. We ourselves must know from our own experience where the 'I Am', or Ego, of humanity truly dwells—in ourselves—and be able to present this 'Ego of Humanity' to the children with dignity and purpose. In this way, the teacher creates a healthy environment in which the child can awaken to the part of his Ego that we are teaching about in the lesson and point to in the outside world. If there is any discrepancy between what the teacher says and what he does, a child of this age will quickly discern it and refuse to accept that teacher's authority and perhaps instruction.

By the age of twenty-one, the birth of the Ego usually has taken place, but the young adult still must be helped and supported. 'Ontogeny recapitulates phylogeny' is a phrase that speaks succinctly of the three "births" or developmental stages that an incarnating child passes through at this stage to become a young adult. The child must relive all the metamorphoses that humanity has gone through, including the birth of the physical body, the etheric body (age seven), and the astral body (age fourteen), until she receives her individually developed Ego (age twenty-one).

Each 'body' has its birth, while each birth has uniquely characteristic influences surrounding it. But even at age twenty-one, the human Ego is still a dawning experience, and the path beyond that point is also governed by seven-year cycles which do not carry such developmental or powerful influences as we find in the 'births' of the physical body, etheric body, astral body, and Ego. However, when a teacher is knowledgeable about these stages of development, he/she is in the position to give aid, strength, and direction, which may help the young person to pass gracefully into adulthood.

Another perspective from which to view the developmental path of the child between the ages of seven and fourteen and one that will give a background for the dynamic that is being addressed in the Waldorf elementary curriculum, is that of reincarnation. Waldorf education has as its cornerstone a deep belief in repeated human earth lives. Without a belief in life before birth, and a firm grounding in the knowledge that the pre-natal world directly relates to the conceptual life of the child, then we as teachers would be blind to the impact of that pre-natal condition; consequently, we could have no psychological understanding of the child's experience. We must also know, as a soul experience, that all deeds of a human being live on beyond death; otherwise, we can know nothing of the true nature of 'deeds of will' which extend into that after-death condition.

From a contemplation of the birth/death continuum of life, we can begin to realize that the birth of the physical body must be understood in the light of reincarnation, which is a key element in the history of the spiritual evolution of humankind. We must be mindful that the child has chosen the body donated by his parents, and that with gestation and birth the child passes through the cosmic evolutionary cycle of transformation from water (amniotic fluid) to air (first breath of life). With the first breath, the child becomes a citizen of the present, but many forces are also rushing to meet her from the past. All that the child had as forces in prenatal life rushed forth to create her body out of the ether body of the Earth. At birth, the child is given a model (hereditary) ether body which guides, forms, regulates, and enlivens the physical substances which constitute the body. As substance is constantly taken in, transformed, and excreted; the ether body, the memory of the bodily form, is performing the vital functions of the physical body during the waking hours of day and rejuvenating it during the sleeping hours of night. Working through the donated hereditary body of a child are hierarchical spiritual beings that rank even to the realm of the Elohim (Spirits of Form, Exusiai), who envelope the child with love and hold the ether body together from birth until approximately age seven. Then the child's own unique ether body begins to take over these functions and the ether body becomes more a personal reflection of the soul-spirit nature of the child.

The model ether body donated by hierarchical spirit beings is part of the activity, in the first three years of life, when the willpower of the child is present to a marked degree. In these primary years, the child learns to stand erect, speak, and conceptualize (make mental pictures/think). These deeds of will are intrinsically human and are essential to Ego consciousness. Christ, through the combined forces of the Spirits of Form, is the spirit responsible for humanities' I/Ego development and evolution. The Spirits of Form are essentially involved with the development of the Ego because they have donated forces that have helped create the possibility for Ego consciousness. The child receives these gifts as part of the spirit of childhood which leads her forward into adult life.

Through an understanding of this spiritual evolution from childhood to adulthood, teachers must be aware that all things which come into contact with the young child have powerful etheric, organ-forming influence. Food, color, light, warmth, movement, sound, music, speech, forms, gesture, and all other aspects of the environment are the resources from which the child's delicate organs are developed. Therefore, it is especially important during the first three years of life that the child has good nutrition and a healthy environment. A very important element of this healthy environment is acceptance of a child's natural development; one should not try, through clever means, to speed the processes of walking, speaking, or intellectual achievement.

Parents and teachers alike, with loving acceptance and encouragement, must let the being of the child speak to them as its nature unfolds.

Natural development from infancy to adulthood can be best understood in terms of certain predictable cycles. From about two years, four months to four years, eight months; the child is in the middle part of the threefold division of the first seven-year cycle. Rhythm, repetition, and feeling are all-important during this time, as healthy feelings develop out of a regular sense of rhythm. However, whenever possible, the music should be soft and written in the pentatonic scale (a simple scale of five notes with no minors) and stories should be told from the heart (memorized).

Also important to the child's conceptual development, at this time, is her relationship to the rhythms of her mother's and father's speech patterns because the forces in speech create the convolutions of the growing brain. The simple repetition of a memorized story has a profound and almost magical effect on the young child. A lullaby can work wonders.

All these elements are part of a healthy environment for a child and provide the necessary atmosphere that will engender a sense of awe and wonder towards life. Implicit in this environmental design is the need to set about making available a model of truly good human relationships, since from birth until age seven imitation and example serve as the overall keynotes. Whatever the child perceives during these years is taken in and imitated. If what she sees is caring and loving relationships, this will engender a sense of reverence and devotion for people everywhere and smooth the path to further growth and development.

The natural tendency of the child to imitate what she sees and hears is an especially important consideration from the late fourth year until age seven because at this stage she is developing thinking abilities. In order to give examples of healthy, living thinking instead of dry intellectualism in the form of letters and numbers, we must keep all our teaching in the realm of living images. We must paint beautiful imaginations for the child to live into with her whole being. The child can easily memorize when her own etheric forces are at work after the age of seven; until then, the child should not be made to crystallize his body with two-dimensional, abstract concepts.

The mental training of a child can be more properly started around the age of seven when the ether body of the child penetrates from the head downward. The signature of this occurrence is the eruption of the second teeth. At this time, memory comes easier to children. Even contemporary researchers know that this is a signal to begin a more formalized intellectual approach in a child's education. When thinking abilities, associated with memory development, start forming the brain, then will-activity should be used to balance the will/metabolic forces.

This birth of the etheric appears from inside the organism and moves towards the periphery in an expanding, uplifting motion much like the muscle activity that raises the child to the upright position. Thus, at this time, movement, especially rhythmic movement as is found in the activity of eurythmy, is needed to help the forces of memory to be properly integrated into the child's muscular system.

The next critical phase of a child's development takes place usually around age twelve to fourteen, although this can depend greatly on the geographic location due to the onset of puberty having such a wide variance in age. At this stage, the astral body, which has been hovering around the child, contracts into the body, marking the period known as adolescence or puberty. Marking this birth of the astral body and the onset of puberty are changes of voice and growth of the skeleton. As any parent or teacher who has witnessed this transformation from childhood to adulthood can attest, this period can be a chaotic one. The astral body, a vehicle used by the Ego of a child, can be aggressive and animal-like; it can also be melodic, warm, and life-giving. To better ensure that the more positive aspects manifest, the child should be encouraged to play musical instruments, as again it is music that can help satisfy the more chaotic energies of adolescence.

Another calming influence at this stage in a child's development, from the birth of the ether body at age seven to the birth of the astral body at around age fourteen, is having a central class teacher who develops a personal relationship with the child and becomes akin to an etheric/astral midwife. A Waldorf teacher is aware that the human is not a finished being at birth; the physical birth is but one of the births that must be carefully and thoughtfully prepared for. The child must be nurtured and cared for throughout the birth of the etheric and astral bodies with all the loving care that the midwife gives to the birthing process of a newborn baby. Only when a teacher realizes his importance in this process of growth and development can he become the awakened artistic teacher that is needed for the foundation of a sound educational process.

Steiner elucidates this crucial role of the teacher in the first chapter of *Study of Man*, Rudolf Steiner, Lecture I, Stuttgart, August 21, 1919, GA 293:

> "The task of education conceived in the spiritual sense is to bring the Soul-Spirit into harmony with the Life-Body. They must come into harmony with one another. They must be attuned to one another; for when the child is born into the physical world, they do not as yet fit one another. The task of the educator, and of the teacher too, is the mutual attunement of these two members."

In using the term Soul-Spirit, Rudolf Steiner is making reference to the threefold Spirit (Spirit-Self, Life-Spirit, and Spirit-Human) and the threefold Soul (Sentient Soul, Mind/Intellectual Soul, and Consciousness/Spiritual Soul); these two trinities work together. The correct penetration of the Soul-Spirit into the Life or Etheric Body of a human being is accomplished through a proper sense of breathing; which, in turn, determines the rhythm of waking and sleeping.

The teacher must keep in mind that until the age of seven, the child is a citizen of two worlds. She is slowly penetrating the world but is not quite on the earth in her fullest capacity. From the age of seven to fourteen, however, the child becomes ready for school, begins to interact more fully with the environment, and eventually, by the end of this seven-year period, she reaches puberty. Only during this developmental stage can we begin to train the child's memory in a systematic way for concepts which she will use in the exterior world. We must remember not to push the child into accepting things she is not quite ready for. This is why the Waldorf pedagogy maps out the developmental stages of children; these stages help us understand the child more fully and work in harmony with the child's natural developmental processes.

There are signposts along the way that enable a teacher to predict what a child is ready to accept. For example, around age seven, we may see the protrusion of the child's second teeth. Before this time, the model etheric body formed the body of the child; after seven, the individualized etheric body of the child begins to take over the functions of the body. The mobile world of archetypes which the child has been living in until now begins to fade. While this indicates that the child's memory is now able to hold the concepts used in grade school, it also marks the waning of childhood.

Two and one-third years later, at the 'nine-year change,' with growth and added weight, come many changes. Until now, the child has been enjoying feelings of levity and lightness and its recognition of the 'I consciousness' has been emanating from the head region; now the home of the Ego drops from the head region through the chest/rhythmic region on its way into the metabolic processes. As the child begins to feel the limits of gravity restricting her body, the 'I,' or 'Ego consciousness,' is also being limited by these same forces as the consciousness drops further from the head into the throat, and then into the chest/rhythmic region. This change initiates a new experience of space in the child. To accommodate these changes and help the child sort out her feelings in this new realm, the teacher again can turn to the harmonizing influences of music by giving the child a musical instrument to play. Other useful strategies to bring space into perspective are geography lessons and Norse myths which use a pseudo-hexameter meter which helps balance the breath with the heart-rhythm.

All of these methods, however, are only effective if the teacher is aware of these changes and responds to the child with warmth and guidance to help the child live in harmony with herself between the forces of gravity and levity.

The 'twelve-year change' is somewhat like the 'nine-year change,' except now the child has become more aware of time and her place in it. History can now be taught in imaginative pictures because the child is gaining the capacity to understand the flow of time. Roman and Medieval times are taught at this stage, and the lasting cultural, legal, and architectural influences of these periods can be deeply experienced by the student.

By age fourteen, as mentioned earlier, the astral body, which has until now lived outside the body, starts to contract into the child, precipitating the onset of puberty. The voice changes, limbs elongate, and sexual glands develop and become active. The higher-level thinking skills concerning cause and effect are now taught in science classes and can readily be comprehended by the child in this phase of development. In fact, many subjects now become possible to understand, whereas before, the child had no inner experience to match the concepts. By this age, temporal sequencing is fully experienced, and modem history lessons begin. The children have learned about many past civilizations, and now they are introduced to modern history. The child has now descended from the archetypal realm into the space/time realm of earth and modern-day consciousness. This development of the individual student recapitulates the development of humanity as a species. Knowing these stages of the development of the Ego in education are very helpful in understanding the overall development of the 'Small I Am' in relationship to the 'Great I Am' of Christ.

The Nature of Christ— the 'I Am'

Light is shed on the nature of the Cosmic Christ in a lecture referenced below by Rudolf Steiner called *Occult Science and Occult Development*. Christ, as the 'Great I Am' member of the Holy Trinity, has gone through the most unique challenges of any of the gods, He has descended into a human body and experienced death. The Deed of the Mystery of Golgotha, plus the prior three Pre-Earthly Deeds of Christ, have aligned Christ with all past, present, and future aspects of human development and spiritual evolution. When you add the Fifth Deed, the Second Coming of Christ in the Etheric Realm, and the subsequent gift of human memory, you can begin to understand that Christ creates the vehicle of memory which holds the continuity of consciousness of the 'I Am' (Ego) between human incarnations. Memory carries the Ego in the reincarnating Manas/Buddhi (Spirit-Self/Life-Spirit) aspects of the human from life to life. The lower earthly Ego is not eternal and acts for a while as a mirror to the three higher Egos in the spiritual world—Spirit-Self, Life-Spirit, Spirit Human or Manas, Budhi, and Atman. The three spiritual Egos, that accumulate an individual's Moral Imaginations, Moral Inspirations, and Moral Intuitions, use the Spirit-Self and Life-Spirit (Manas/Budhi) to create the personal memory imprinted in the Akashic Records from lifetime to lifetime. This creates the karmic spiritual biography of the individual that gives the person their distinctiveness to add to the Group-Soul of Christened Beings. This continuity of memory is the basis for the immortal 'I Am' to take up residence in the three higher Egos and is another gift of Christ given to humanity since

His incarnation in Palestine. If we also add the most current gift of Christ, the redemption and resurrection of the etheric realm around the Earth and in the human etheric body, we see that another Christ-deed and sacrifice is happening in our own time. Dr. Steiner told us that the 'Second Coming of Christ in the Etheric Realm' is the second greatest event of human history. This mighty etheric crucifixion and resurrection is yet another 'Deed' of Christ that directly affects the human Ego's development by giving the spiritual aspirant a chance to meet Christ in the etheric realm as an Angel, with the help of the Nathan Jesus (Adam Kadmon) who appears as an Angel in the astral light. Once again, the Nathan Jesus links with Christ and human development to help raise all spiritual boats through a new 'tide' of etheric life provided by Christ.

As we can see, Rudolf Steiner's Cosmology of Christ is the most comprehensive picture of the biography of the 'Great I Am' found anywhere. Let's hear how Steiner describes the unique nature of Christ in: *Occult Science and Occult Development,* Rudolf Steiner, Lecture II, *Christ at the Time of the Mystery of Golgotha and Christ in the Twentieth Century,* May 2, 1913, GA 152:

> "There is no death for any of the Beings belonging to the higher Hierarchies, with the one exception of Christ. But in order that a super-sensible Being such as Christ should be able to pass through death, He must first have descended to the earth. And the fact of immeasurable significance in the Mystery of Golgotha is that a Being who in the realm of His own will could never have experienced death, should have descended to the earth in order to undergo an experience connected inherently with man. Thereby that inner bond was created between earthly mankind and Christ, in that this Being passed through death in order to share this destiny with man. As I have already emphasized, that death was of the greatest possible importance, above all for the present evolutionary

period of the earth. A Being of unique nature who until then was only cosmic, was united with the earth's evolution through the Mystery of Golgotha, through Christ's death. At the time of the Mystery of Golgotha, He entered into the very process of the earth's evolution. This had not been the case before that event, for He then belonged to the Cosmos alone; but through the Mystery of Golgotha, He descended out of the Cosmos and was incorporated on earth. Since then, He lives on the earth, is united with the earth in such a way that He lives within the souls of men and with them experiences life on the earth. Thus, the whole period before the Mystery of Golgotha was only a time of preparation in the evolution of the earth. The Mystery of Golgotha imparted to the earth its meaning and purpose."

"When the Mystery of Golgotha took place the earthly body of Jesus of Nazareth was given over to the elements of the earth, and from that time onwards Christ has been united with the spiritual sphere of the earth and lives within it. For three years after the Baptism in the Jordan, Christ lived in the body of Jesus of Nazareth as a man among men of the earth. This may be called the earthly manifestation of Christ in a physical, human body."

"We must naturally think of the Christ Being as a stupendously lofty Being, but although He is so sublime, He was nevertheless able, during the three years after the Baptism, to express Himself in a human body. But in what form does He reveal Himself since that time? No longer in the physical body, for that was given over to the physical earth and is now part of it. To those who through the study of occult science have developed the power to see into these things, it will be revealed that this Being can be recognized in one belonging to the Hierarchy of the Angels. Just as the Savior of the world manifested Himself during the three years after the Baptism in a human body—in spite of His sublimity—so, since that time, He manifests Himself directly as an Angel, as a spiritual Being belonging to the hierarchical rank immediately above that of mankind. As such, He could always be found by those who were clairvoyant, as such, He has always been united with evolution. Just as truly as Christ, when incarnated in the body of Jesus of Nazareth, was more than man, so is the Christ Being more than an Angel—that is His outer form only."

"When such a Being takes on a human or an Angelic form, He Himself progresses. And it is this that we have indicated in speaking of the evolution of Christ-Jehovah. Christ has reached the stage where He reveals Himself henceforth not as a human being, not through His reflection only, not through the name of Jehovah, but directly. And the great difference in all the teachings and all the wisdom that have streamed into the evolution of the earth since the Mystery of Golgotha, is that through the coming of Michael—the Spirit Michael—to the earth, through his inspiration, man could gradually begin to understand all that the Christ Impulse, all that the Mystery of Golgotha signifies. But in that earlier time Michael was the messenger of Jehovah, the reflection of the light of Christ; he was not yet the messenger of Christ Himself…"

"…The 'seeds of earthly materialism' which were increasingly carried into the spiritual world by the souls who went through the portal of death since the sixteenth century, and which caused more and more darkness, built the 'black sphere of materialism.' Christ took this black sphere into being in the sense of the Manichean principle for the purpose of transforming it. For the Angel being in which the Christ had manifested himself since the Mystery of Golgotha the black sphere caused a 'death by suffocation.' This sacrifice by Christ in the nineteenth century is comparable to the sacrifice on the physical plane through the Mystery of Golgotha and can be called the second crucifixion of Christ on the etheric plane. This spiritual death by suffocation, which brought about the extinction of the consciousness of the Angelic Being is a repetition of the Mystery of Golgotha in those worlds that lie immediately behind our world. It took place to make possible a revival of the Christ consciousness which was earlier hidden in human souls on earth. The revival becomes clairvoyant vision for humanity in the twentieth century."

"Thus, the Christ-consciousness may be united with the earthly consciousness of men from our time on into the future; for the dying of the Christ consciousness in the sphere of the Angels in the nineteenth century signifies the resurrection of the direct consciousness of Christ—that is to say, Christ's life will be felt in the souls of men more and more as a direct personal experience from the twentieth century onwards."

"Twice already Christ has been crucified: once physically, in the physical world at the beginning of our era, and a second time spiritually, in the nineteenth century, in the way described above. It could be said that mankind experienced the resurrection of His body in that former time and will experience the resurrection of His consciousness from the twentieth century onwards."

Buddha and Christ: The Sphere of the Bodhisattvas, Rudolf Steiner, Lecture in Milan, September 21, 1911, GA 130

"In our own Fifth Age which will last until the fourth millennium, souls will gradually become able, from the 20th century onwards, to experience the Christ Being in an etheric form on the astral plane, just as in the fourth age Christ was visible on the physical plane in a physical form. What is meant by 'an etheric form on the astral plane?' The astral body is the body of desires, wishes, passions, fantasies, originality, creativity, etc., and to the extent that the Ego and the intellectual soul effectively work on this surging, colorful, and dynamic body so as to bring it under control, its forces are transformed into Spirit-Self (Manas), which means elevated, moral thinking, pure or untainted thoughts. This kind of thinking will enable a 'face to face' meeting with Christ and with other higher Beings, which can mean a vision full of truth, a vision that is almost physical, but that is not physical. Elements of unmistakable life and sweetness identify the vision as originating from the etheric world, but pure thoughts (correct thinking) within the intellectual soul must facilitate this meeting so long as humanity is dependent upon the physical body and physical life. This dependency will continue for a long time into the future but must ultimately be overcome."

The Great 'I Am' Throughout History

A short list of gods, heroes, myths, avatars, and saviors are enumerated below. As we can see, these deities, or 'divine humans,' exist in almost every culture and span the scope of recorded history. It is instructive to study these 'predictions' of the Pre-Earthly Deeds of Christ in pre-Christian times. Each of these natural clairvoyant perceptions of a god or deity working for the good of humanity out of the realm of the Sun is just another confirmation that atavistic clairvoyants of the past were actively perceiving Christ descending from the Sun to the Earth with the mission to help all 'Small I Am(s)' grow into the 'Great I Am'—a perfect model of the divine provided by Christ and the perfect model of the human being provided by Adam Kadmon (Nathan Jesus). Evidence of prior solar saviors are not a diminishing or dismissal of Jesus Christ, but are a confirmation that the world was waiting on Christ and could directly perceive Him in the rays of Sun and in His Pre-Earthly Deeds.

The crown jewel of the human being is the 'I Am' (Ego) which is given to us by Christ. Many stories tell of this gift and its significance for the saviors of humanity to create and nourish. This 'little Ego' of humanity is a seedling in the garden of the Cosmos, but each seed has the capacity to grow into a 'World Tree.'

Here is a list of beings, heroes, gods, and myths that indicate that the 'I Am', and its care and sustenance, is the primal concern of gods and goddesses:

Krishna of Hindustan, Bali of Afghanistan, Jao of Nepaul, Salivahana of Bermuda, Wittoba of the Bilingo, Zulis, Osiris of Egypt, Thammuz of Syria, Odin of the Scandinavi, Attis of Phrygia, Xamolxis of Thrace, Crite of Chaldea, Zoar of the Bonzes Zoroaster, Mithra of Persia, Adad of Assyria, Deva Tat, Sammono, Baal, Taut, Alcides of Thebes, Phenicia, Mikado of the Sintoos, Indra of Thibet, Beddru of Japan, Hesus or Eros, Brem rillah of the Druids, Thor son of Odin, Cadmus of Greece, Gentaut and Quexalcote of Mexico, Universal Monarch of the Sibyls, Ischy of the Island of Formosa, Divine Teacher of Plato, Holy One of Xaca, Fohi and Tien of China, Adonis son of Io of Greece, Ixion and Quirinus of Rome, Prometheus of Caucasus.

Ancient India

Tvashtar (Ishvara)—The Vedic Tvashtar was the great architect and artisan. Ishvara is the Supreme Self, ruler, lord, king, queen, or husband. In Hindu texts, Ishvara (Tvashtar) is God, Supreme Being, personal God, or special Self—the OM. Ishvara is often depicted as female and the mother of all other deities and is sometimes seen as Vishvakarman. Tvashtar gave being to all things and is the God, the omni-form creator, who begets and feeds humanity in various manners. Even in the womb the God Tvastar, the Vivifier, shaping all forms, Creator, made us consorts. None violates his/her holy ordinances: that we are hers/his, the heavens and earth acknowledge.

Vishvakarman—From the *Upanishads* and the Vedas we know that Brahman and Atman are the same, one is the 'I Am' of the Cosmos while the other is the 'I Am' of the human individual. There are many other names for both of these beings. Brahman is also called Ishvara. In the Puranas, Tvashtar and Vishvakarman are different just as they are in the Vedas. Sanjna, the daughter of Vishvakarman, was the wife of the Sun, and bore him three children, the Manu, Yama, and the goddess Yami. The Vedic Vishvakarman was God the Creator, the Supreme God, like Brahman, since He is the one who creates everything, a job that the Puranas give to Brahma. Vishvakarman "who hath eyes on all sides round about him, a mouth on all sides, arms and feet on all sides, He, the Sole God, producing earth and heaven, weldeth them, with his arms as wings, together. The Father of the eye, the Wise in spirit, created both these worlds submerged in fastness. Then, when the eastern ends were firmly fastened, the heavens and the earth were far extended."

The East in the Light of the West, Rudolf Steiner, Lecture VI, Munich August 28, 1909, GA 113

"When the holy Rishis of antiquity looked up into the spiritual worlds they spoke of Vishvakarman, who was the same cosmic being to whom Zoroaster referred when he spoke of Ahura Mazdao. It was the Christ Being."

Krishna of India, 1200 BC—Krishna is one of the most widely revered and most popular of all Indian divinities, worshipped as the eighth incarnation (avatar) of the Hindu god Vishnu and also as a supreme god in his own right. Krishna became the focus of numerous bhakti (devotional) cults, which have over the centuries produced a wealth of religious poetry, music, and painting. The child Krishna was adored for his mischievous pranks; he also performed many miracles and slew demons. As the god sat in the forest lamenting, a huntsman, mistaking him for a deer, shot him in his one vulnerable spot, the heel, killing him. His worship preserved distinctive traits, chief among them an exploration of the analogies between divine love and human love.

***The Bhagavad Gita and the Epistles of St. Paul*, Rudolf Steiner, Lecture III, Cologne, December 30, 1912, GA 142**

"From time-to-time Beings appear for the guidance of mankind such as we look up to in Krishna, the Great Teacher of Arjuna. Krishna teaches the highest human wisdom, the highest humanity, and he teaches it as being his own nature, and also in such a way that it is related to every human being, for all that is contained in the words of Krishna is to be found in germ in every human soul."

"Arjuna was uplifted suddenly at a bound, as it were, so that bodily he has Krishna before him; and the Gita leads up to a definite. point, the point at which Krishna stood before him. "The rest of the world disappears and Krishna is there as ONE. As the macrocosm to the microcosm, as mankind, as a whole, compared to the small everyday man, so is Krishna to the individual man."

***The Occult Significance of the Bhagavad Gita*, Rudolf Steiner, Lecture IX, Helsingfors, June 5, 1913, GA 146**

"Krishna—that is, the spirit who worked through Krishna— appeared again in the Jesus child of the Nathan line of the House of David, described in *St. Luke's Gospel*. Thus, fundamentally, this child embodied the impulse, all the forces that tend to make man independent and loosen him from external reality. What was the intention of this soul that did not enter human evolution but worked in Krishna and again in this Jesus child? At a far distant time this soul had had to go through the experience of remaining outside human evolution because the antagonist Lucifer had come; he who said, 'Your eyes will be opened and you will distinguish good and evil and be as God.' In the ancient Indian sense Lucifer said to man, 'You will be as the Gods, and will have power to find the Sattva, Rajas and Tamas conditions in the world.'"

The Occult Significance of the Bhagavad Gita, Rudolf Steiner, Lecture IX, Helsingfors, June 5, 1913, GA 146

"Lucifer directed man's attention to the outer world. By his instigation man had to learn to know the external, and therefore had to go through the long course of evolution down to the time of Christ. Then he came who was once withdrawn from Lucifer; came in Krishna and later in the Luke Jesus child. In two stages he gave that teaching that from another side was to be the antithesis of the teaching of Lucifer in Paradise."

Lord Surya—Indic Rigveda have solar divinities that are not distinct from Mithra and are associated with the Sunrise in the Atharvaveda. Sun Salutation is a daily yogic activity worldwide even in current times and is preceded by chanting "OM Maitreya Namaha", where "Maitreya" is one of the 108 Names for Lord Surya/Sun God.

***Indra of Tibet**, 725 BC*—Plates representing this Tibetan savior as having been nailed to the cross may be found in Georgius, *Thibetinum Alphabetum*. There are five wounds, representing the nail-holes and the piercing of the side. He descended from heaven on a mission of benevolence and ascended back to the heavenly mansion after his crucifixion. He led a life of strict celibacy, which, he taught, was essential to true holiness. He inculcated great tenderness towards all living beings. He could walk upon the water or upon the air; could foretell future events with great accuracy. He practiced the most devout contemplation, severe discipline of the body and mind, and acquired the most complete subjection of his passions. He was worshiped as a god who had existed as a spirit from all eternity.

Ancient Persia

Ahura Mazda—While fetching water at dawn for a sacred ritual, he saw the shining figure of the Amesha Spenta, Vohu Manah, who led Zoroaster to the presence of Ahura Mazda, where he was taught the cardinal principles of the "Good Religion" later known as Zoroastrianism. As a result of this vision, Zoroaster felt that he was chosen to spread and preach the religion. He stated that this source of all goodness was the Ahura worthy of the highest worship. He further stated that Ahura Mazda created spirits known as yazatas to aid him. Zoroaster proclaimed that some of the Iranian gods were devas who deserved no worship. These "bad" deities were created by Angra Mainyu, the destructive spirit. The existence of Angra Mainyu was the source of all sin and misery in the universe. Zoroaster claimed that Ahura Mazda was not an omnipotent God, but used the aid of humans in the cosmic struggle against Angra Mainyu. Nonetheless, Ahura Mazda is Angra Mainyu's superior, not his equal. Angra Mainyu and his devas, which attempt to attract humans away from the Path of Asha, would eventually be defeated.

The Gospel of St. Luke, **Rudolf Steiner, Lecture VII. Basel September 21, 1909, GA 114**

"The [ancient Indian] Rishis taught of the Being whom they called 'Vishvakarman' and Zarathustra called 'Ahura Mazdao.' Vishvakarman and Ahura Mazdao were two of the names for this Being who was gradually approaching the Earth from heights of spirit, from cosmic realms."

"All spiritual science, all our wisdom, all our knowledge, must be devoted to understanding the nature of Vishvakarman, of Ahura Mazdao, of CHRIST.

Egypt/Chaldea/Sumeria

Isis, Osiris, and Horus—The Osiris myth is the most elaborate and influential story in ancient Egyptian mythology. It concerns the murder of the god Osiris, a primeval king of Egypt, and its consequences. Osiris's murderer, his brother Set, usurps his throne. Meanwhile, Osiris's wife Isis restores her husband's body, allowing him to posthumously conceive their son, Horus. The remainder of the story focuses on Horus, the product of the union of Isis and Osiris, who is at first a vulnerable child protected by his mother and then becomes Set's rival for the throne. Their often violent conflict ends with Horus's triumph, which restores Maat (cosmic and social order) to Egypt after Set's unrighteous reign.

Isis—Near the Temple of Isis at Sais was the "grave of Osiris," where the Osirian Mysteries were carried out. Greek visitors to Sais such as Herodotus, Plato, and Diodorus Siculus identified this Neith-Isis with Athena, holding that Athena built the city before she founded Athens, and that when Athens and Atlantis were destroyed by the great flood, Sais survived. Thus, the triple Goddess Neith-Isis-Athena was worshiped at the goddess's shrine at Sais, a combination of very ancient feminine divinities. This ties together the universality of the divinity of Isis—consonant with her identity with Neith—the Primordial Source of all that is, with the evocative symbol of the Veil of Isis, concealing unglimpsed mysteries. It is that symbol, the Veil covering the Source of All from our gaze, that has inspired philosophers, mystics, and artists for two millennia. Proclus tells us in his Commentary on the Timaeus that Isis has declared: "I am what is, and what will be, and what has been, no one has lifted my veil. The fruit I bore was the Sun."

Thulis of Egypt, 1700 BC—He died the death of the cross about thirty-five hundred years ago. Ultima Thule was the island which marked the ultimate bounds of the extensive empire of this legitimate descendant of the gods. This Egyptian Savior appears also to have been known as Zulis. We are told twenty-eight lotus plants near his grave indicate the number of years he lived on the earth. After suffering a violent death, he was buried, but rose again, ascended into heaven, and there became 'the judge of the dead.' Thulis came down from heaven to benefit mankind, and he was said to be full of grace and truth.

Tammuz—The cult of Ishtar and Tammuz continued to thrive until the eleventh century AD and survived in parts of Mesopotamia as late as the eighteenth century. Tammuz was widely seen as a prime example of the archetypal dying-and-rising god. Tammuz or Dumuzi, is an ancient Mesopotamian god associated with shepherds, who was also the primary consort of the goddess Inanna (Ishtar). In Inanna's Descent into the Underworld, Dumuzi fails to mourn Inanna's death and, when she returns from the Underworld, she allows the demons to drag him down to the Underworld as her replacement. Inanna later regrets this decision and decrees that Dumuzi will spend half the year in the Underworld, but the other half of the year with her, while his sister Geshtinanna stays in the Underworld in his place, thus resulting in the cycle of the seasons.

Shamash/Utu—He was later worshipped by the East Semitic Akkadian-speaking Babylonians as Shamash. He was the ancient

Mesopotamian Sun god; god of justice, morality, and truth, and the twin of the Mesopotamian goddess Inanna (Ishtar in the Assyrio-Babylonian language), the Queen of Heaven. He was believed to ride through the heavens in his Sun chariot and see all that happened in the day. He was the enforcer of divine justice and was thought to aid those in distress.

Attis of Phrygia, 1170 BC—Attis was the mythical consort of the Great Mother of the Gods Cybele. He was worshipped in Phrygia, Asia Minor, and later throughout the Roman Empire, where he was made a solar deity in the 2nd century AD. The worship of Attis and the Great Mother included the annual celebration of mysteries on the return of the spring season. Attis was a beautiful youth who was fundamentally a vegetation god, and in his self-mutilation, death, and resurrection he represents the fruits of the earth, which die in winter only to rise again in the spring.

Crite of Chaldea, 1200 BC—The Chaldeans have noted in their sacred books the account of the crucifixion of a God with the name Crite. He was also known as "the Redeemer," and was styled "the Ever-Blessed Son of God," "the Savior of the Race," "the Atoning Offering for an Angry God." And when he was offered up, both heaven and earth were shaken to their foundations.

Norse Mythology

Odin of the Scandinavians—Many early scholars interpreted him as a wind-god or especially as a death-god. He has also been interpreted in the light of his association with ecstatic practices and compared to the Hindu god Rudra and the Greek Hermes. Norse mythology, the source of most surviving information about him, generally portrays Odin as king of the gods and associates him with wisdom, healing, death, royalty, the gallows, knowledge, war, battle, victory, sorcery, poetry, frenzy, and the runic alphabet, and depicts him as the husband of the goddess Frigg. Odin was crucified by himself on the world tree, Yggdrasil. Poetic Edda: "I know that I hung on a wind-rocked tree, nine whole nights, with a spear wounded, and to Odin offered, myself to myself; on that tree, of which no one knows, from what root it springs. Bread no one gave me, nor a horn of drink, downward I peered, to runes applied myself, wailing learnt them, then fell down thence."

The Mission of Folk-Souls, Rudolf Steiner, Lecture VIII. The five Post-Atlantean Civilizations. Greek and Teutonic Mythology, Christiania (Oslo), June 14, 1910, GA 121

"In the first place he beheld the Archangelic Beings who worked in his soul and endowed him with his psychic potentialities, and the greatest of these Archangels was Wotan or Odin. He saw him at work upon his soul and he saw how he worked into his soul. How did he perceive Wotan or Odin?"

Baldur—He is the second son of Odin who is the best of the gods, and all praised him; he is so fair of feature, and so bright, that light shines from him. He is the wisest of the Aesir, and the fairest-spoken and most gracious. He dwells in the place called Breidablik, which is in heaven; in that place 'may nothing unclean be.' Baldur is known for the story of his death, which leads to the destruction of the gods at Ragnarok. Frigg made every object on earth vow never to hurt Baldur. All objects made this vow except the mistletoe. Loki made a magical arrow from this plant and hurried to the place where the gods were indulging in their new pastime of hurling objects at Baldur, which would bounce off without harming him due to the oaths they made. Loki gave the spear to Baldur's brother, the blind god Hoder, who then inadvertently threw it at Baldur and it killed him. Upon Frigg's entreaties, Hel promised to release Baldur from the underworld if all objects alive and dead would weep for him. All did, except for Loki who was disguised as a giantess who refused to mourn the slain god. Thus, Baldur had to remain in the underworld, not to emerge until after Ragnarok when he and his brother Hoder would be reconciled and rule the new earth together with Thor's sons. (See Diagram IV)

Celtic

Hesus, 834 BC—He is the Celtic-Druid's Sun savior, closely associated to Jupiter or Zeus. He was born December 25th to a virgin mother Mayence, fathered by Gudt the Sun deity. Hesus or Esus Crios was a healing savior, also known as the deity of vegetation. He was regarded by the Romans as Mercury or Mithra. Esus was the third being in the Celtic trinity. Hesus died on the cross; a lamb on one side, which symbolized his innocence, and elephant on the side, which signified the sins of the world he came to redeem.

Finnish Kalevala

Vainamoinen—The 50th and final poem of the *Kalevala* tells the story of the maiden Marjatta, who becomes pregnant after eating a berry and subsequently giving birth to a baby boy. This child is brought to Vainamoinen, the old singer of creation, to examine and judge. His verdict is that such a strangely born infant needs to be put to death. In reply, the newborn child, merely two weeks old, chides the old sage for his sins and transgressions, such as allowing the maiden Aino, sister of Joukahainen to drown herself. Following this, the baby is baptized and named king of Kalevala. Defeated, Vainamoinen goes to the shores of the sea, where he sings for himself a boat of copper with which he sails away from the mortal realms. In his final words, he promises that there shall be a time when he shall return, when his crafts and might shall once again be needed. The 50th poem thus echoes the arrival of Christianity to Finland and the subsequent fading into history of the old pagan beliefs and the creator himself, Vainamoinen.

Hebrew

Messiah—A messiah in Abrahamic religions is a savior of the people. In Judaism and in the Hebrew Bible a mashiach is a king or High Priest anointed with holy anointing oil physically descended from the line of King David and King Solomon. The Greek translation of Messiah is Khristos, anglicized as Christ. Christians commonly refer to Jesus of Nazareth as either the "Christ" or the "Messiah", believing that the messianic prophecies were fulfilled in the mission, death, and resurrection of Jesus and that he will return to fulfill the rest of messianic prophecies. Unlike the Judaic concept of the Messiah, Jesus Christ is additionally considered by Christians to be the Son of God. In Islam, Jesus is held to have been a prophet and the Messiah sent to the Israelites, who will return to Earth at the end of times along with the Mahdi, and defeat the false messiahs.

Greek

Helios—He is the son of Hyperion and Theia. Homer in the *Odyssey* calls him Helios Hyperion ("the Sun, up above"). Later poets distinguish between Helios and Hyperion as distinctly father and son. Helios is usually depicted as a handsome young man crowned with the shining aureole of the Sun who drove the chariot of the Sun across the sky each day to Earth-circling Oceanus and through the world-ocean returned to the East at night. The imagery surrounding a chariot-driving solar deity is likely Indo-European in origin and is common to both early Greek and Near Eastern religions. The earliest artistic representations of the "chariot god" come from the Parthian period (3rd century) in Persia where there is evidence of rituals being performed for the Sun god by Magi, indicating an assimilation of the worship of Helios and Mithras. Helios is seen as both a personification of the Sun and the fundamental creative power behind it and as a result is often worshiped as a god of life and creation.

Dionysus—In the Orphic tradition, Dionysus was, in part, a god associated with the underworld. As a result, the Orphics considered him the son of Persephone, and believed that he had been dismembered by the Titans and then reborn. The myth of the dismemberment of Dionysus was alluded to as early as the fourth century BC by Plato in his *Phaedo*, in which Socrates claims that the initiations of the Dionysian Mysteries are similar to those of the philosophic path. In Olympian tradition, Zeus had intercourse with Persephone in the form of a serpent, producing Dionysus. The infant was taken to Mount Ida, where, like the infant Zeus, he was guarded by the dancing Curetes. Zeus intended Dionysus to be his successor as ruler of the Cosmos, but a jealous Hera incited the Titans to kill the child. Dionysus is also said to be the son of Zeus and Demeter, the goddess of agriculture. Dionysus, god of the vine, was born from the gods of the rain and the earth. He was torn apart and boiled by the Titans symbolizing the harvesting and wine-making process. Just as the remains of the bare vines are returned to the earth to restore its fruitfulness, the remains of the young Dionysus were returned to Demeter allowing him to be born again.

Adonis—He was a great hunter and Artemis got jealous of his hunting skills and sent a wild boar which eventually killed Adonis in one of his hunting expeditions. A different version of the myth has it that the boar was sent by Ares, as he was the lover of Aphrodite. Adonis bled to death in Aphrodite's arms. Anemones sprang out of the tears of Aphrodite while she was mourning the death of her lover.

Alcestos of Euripides, 600 BC—*The English Classical Journal* (vol-xxxvii) furnishes us with the story of another crucified deity, known as Alcestos, who was a female goddess; and in this respect, somewhat of a novelty in sacred history being such an excellent example of a feminine god atoning for the sins of the world upon the cross. The doctrine of the trinity and the atoning offering for sin was inculcated as a part of her religion.

Iao of Nepaul, 622 BC—Iao was crucified on a tree in Nepaul according to *Georgius* (p. 202). The name of this incarnate God and oriental savior occurs frequently in the holy bibles and sacred books of other countries.

Aeschylus Prometheus of Caucasus, 547 BC—He was nailed to an upright beam of timber, to which were affixed extended arms of wood. This cross was placed near the Caspian Straits where Prometheus was crucified on a Scythian crag for his sin of "loving mortals." Thomas Taylor makes the statement in his *Syntagma*, that the whole story of Prometheus' crucifixion, burial, and resurrection was acted in pantomime in Athens five hundred years before Christ.

Roman

Mithra of Persia, 600 BC—In Zoroastrian tradition, Mithra evolved from being an all-seeing figure into a divinity co-identified with the Sun itself, effectively taking over Hvare-khshaeta's role. It is uncertain why this occurred, but it is commonly attributed to conflation with the Babylonian Sun God Shamash and/or the Greek deity Apollo, with whom Mithra shares being a judge of humanity and steward of the Sun. Royal names incorporating Mithra appear in the dynasties of Parthia, Armenia, Anatolia, Pontus, and Cappadocia. The youthful Apollonian-type Mithra is found in images from other countries also.

From Jesus to Christ, **Rudolf Steiner, Karlsruhe. October 4, 1911, GA 69c**

"The teaching consisted in showing that what was hidden in external nature (Mithra) as also in the inner man of the Greek, poured through the world as a stream of divine consecration. "The God Who could now penetrate into the human soul (neither as Mithra from without, nor Dionysius from within) was Himself a fusion of Mithra and Dionysius, and also was related to human nature in its depths."

"Through the fact that the human gaze was guided to Jesus of Nazareth in Whom Mithra lived and Who then passed through death, an indication was given that Mithra (the bestower of courage, self-control, and energy) had Himself died with the death of Jesus."

Wittoba of the Telingonese, 552 BC—He is represented in history with nail-holes in his hands and the soles of his feet. Nails, hammers, and pincers are constantly seen represented on his crucifixes and are objects of adoration among his followers. The worship of this crucified savior prevails chiefly in the Travancore and other southern Countries in the region of Madura.

Quirinus of Rome, 506 BC—He is represented as having been conceived and brought forth by a virgin; his life was sought by the reigning king; he was of royal blood; he was "put to death by wicked hands" through crucifixion; during his death the whole earth is said to have been enveloped in darkness; and he is said to have resurrected and ascended back to heaven.

Americas

Quezalcoatl of Mexico, 587 BC—Whose name may be translated as "plumed serpent" or "precious twin", was a great Mesoamerican god. He was also a culture hero, a legendary figure who represents the ideals of a cultural group. As a god, Quetzalcoatl was worshiped by early peoples of pre-Hispanic Mexico and Central America, including the Toltec and the Aztec who succeeded them in central Mexico. Quetzalcoatl was a creator god and a wind god. He also was associated with learning, with the Aztec zodiac, and with fertility, water, and vegetation. As a culture hero, Quetzalcoatl taught humankind how to make arts and crafts and measure time. One myth describes how Quetzalcoatl and his three brothers, including Tezcatlipoca, were given the task of creating the world. At first, they cooperated, making fire, the heavens, the waters, a great fish whose flesh became Earth, and half a Sun. The half-Sun did not give enough light, so Tezcatlipoca decided to transform himself into a Sun. A long struggle followed, with the brothers knocking each other out of the sky and placing different deities there as the Sun. After causing great destruction with fire, floods, rampaging giants, and a tornado—and collapsing the heavens themselves—the brothers finally reconciled, repaired the damage, and created a new Sun by sacrificing Quetzalcoatl's son.

Mani, 242 AD—Mani was born in the Babylonian district of Nahr Kutha. His father was a member of a Jewish Christian sect and Mani was raised in a heterodox environment in Babylon. At ages 12 and 24 Mani had visionary experiences of a "heavenly twin" of his (syzygos), calling him to leave his father's sect and preach the true message of Jesus in a new gospel. Mani then travelled to India and studied Hinduism and Buddhism. Returning in 242 AD, Mani presented himself to Shapur I, to whom he dedicated his only work written in Persian, known as the *Shabuhragan*, a mixture of Christianity, Buddhism and Zoroastrianism. Shapur was not converted to Manichaeism but favored Mani's teachings which he brought into his court. Mani is said to have performed miracles, including levitation, teleporting, and healing and was also famed as a painter. Bahram I persecuted the Manichaeans and incarcerated Mani, who died in prison within a month, in 274 AD. Mani's followers depicted Mani's death as a crucifixion in a conscious analogy to the crucifixion of Jesus.

Rudolf Steiner on the Pre-Earthly Deeds of Christ

Through the Pre-Earthly Deeds of Christ, humans became able to stand erect, speak, and think. Christ brought with Him to Earth the 'Ego capacity to think as a free being' and through the Mystery of Golgotha donated the Ego to humanity as His Fourth Deed, of the major Seven Deeds of Christ we are enumerating in this book. In our time, Christ is renewing the etheric body of humanity so that it will continue to have eternal life. Christ is found intimately in every part of the human physical constitution because He is the divine archetype of the human being. Christ grows along with humanity. Christ was always to be found, even in ancient times, working from the spiritual world to help His children. It is Christ who, even before man appeared on Earth, sent down the laws of karma to Earth and mitigated humanity's evolution through His Pre-Earthly Deeds. Then, Christ came to the Earth incarnating in a human being at the Baptism in order to conquer death and bestow conscious eternal life on the faithful.

    Rudolf Steiner has told us about what was accomplished by Christ in the Earthly etheric sphere and the significance of the Event of Golgotha and its effect also upon those who, at that time, were within the spiritual world; and therefore, not incarnated in earthly bodies. At the moment on Golgotha when Christ's blood flowed from His wounds, Christ appeared within the underworld to redeem the dead and He also flooded Spirit-Land with radiant light, universal wisdom, and undying love. The appearance of Christ on the Earth through the Mystery of Golgotha is an event of supreme importance for humanity's evolution, and also for the dead and the realms that humanity passes through between death and a new birth. The incarnation of Christ was even a transformative event for the nine orders of Divine Spiritual Hierarchies above mankind; for they had no direct knowledge or experience of this world of earthly death.

These Pre-Earthly Deeds of Christ are exclusively elaborated upon by Rudolf Steiner and stand as one of the most incredible insights about the nature of the Cosmic Christ that can be found in any Christian cosmology. These profound insights are only equaled by Dr. Steiner's gift of *The Fifth Gospel* which illuminates the missing years of Jesus of Nazareth and the mystery wisdom of the Cosmic Christ found in the other *Gospels*. With these insights of Steiner's, we can begin to fill in many of the missing pieces to the biography of the 'Great I Am' and its child the 'Small I Am.'

Background of the Mystery of Golgotha, Rudolf Steiner, Lecture VII, *Pre-Earthly Deeds of Christ,* Pforzheim, March 7, 1914, GA 152

"It has been said repeatedly, and is well known to you, that in preparation for the Mystery of Golgotha two Jesus-children were born. The one was the Jesus who descended from the line of Solomon and bore the Ego of Zarathustra. The other, coming from the Nathan line of the House of David, was a very special Being. In the twelfth year of the life of the latter the Ego of Zarathustra passed over into him from the child of the line of Solomon, and from that time until his thirtieth year the Nathan child with the Ego of Zarathustra made himself ready to receive the Christ-Being. This event is indicated through the Baptism in Jordan when Jesus of Nazareth was permeated by the Christ Being. At His death the Christ-Being poured Himself out into the spiritual Earth-sphere, so that mankind may become more and more able to participate in that which, proceeding from the Mystery of Golgotha, can pour forth spiritual forces into the souls and hearts of all men."

"In a certain sense, as preparation, this Mystery had already been accomplished three times before for the salvation of mankind: once in the old Lemurian Epoch, then in the Atlantean, and once again at the end of Atlantean times. That is, three times and then a fourth time in the Post-Atlantean Epoch at the beginning of our own era. That which we know as the Mystery of Golgotha, however, was the only one enacted on the physical plane. The other events, which were preparatory, took place wholly in the spiritual world; but the forces which were thus developed flowed down into the earthly souls and bodies for the salvation of mankind. In all three of these preparatory events that same Being was present who was born later as the Nathan-Jesus and who was permeated by the Christ-being. This is the essential fact in the Mystery of Golgotha that the Jesus Being who grew up as the Nathan boy was permeated by the Christ-being. He who was later the Nathan-Jesus had been present in the three earlier events, but not incarnated as physical man; he lived in the spiritual worlds as a spiritual Being of the nature of the Archangels; and in the spiritual worlds, in the preparatory stages of the Mystery of Golgotha, in the Lemurian Epoch and twice in Atlantis, he was permeated by the Christ-Being."

"It may be said, therefore, that there were three Archangel-lives in the spiritual world, and that the Being who lived those lives was the same as he who was later incarnated as man and is described in the *Gospel of St. Luke* as the Jesus-child. Three times had this Angelic being, who later sacrificed himself as Man, offered himself for permeation by the Christ-impulse. As in Christ Jesus, we have a Man permeated with the Christ-impulse, so it may be said that three times previously we have an Angel permeated with that Impulse. And as that which was accomplished by the Mystery of Golgotha streamed forth into the spiritual atmosphere of the Earth, so did that which was brought about by the first three events pour into the Earth from out the Cosmos. Looking at the course of our human evolution we note that the Mystery of Golgotha stands in its very center. Everything that went before was in preparation for and pointed to this Event, which was the center-point of human development, and everything that has since happened is a gradual advance in the streaming of the forces of the Mystery into the hearts and souls of men."

"Three things, which I have pointed out in former lectures, precede the awakening of the Ego in the child—three things of immense importance. The child learns to walk; that is to say, he learns to raise himself from the position in which he was incapable of lifting his body from the earth level towards the heavenly heights of the Cosmos. He is now in that position which, above all, distinguishes man from the animals. Having learnt by his own inner forces to assume it, he turns his gaze away from the earth at which the animal is compelled to look by reason of its nature and form."

"It is this upright position that the child learns to acquire before the awakening of his Ego-consciousness. In our present post-Atlantean life we recapitulate those things which, as man, we have acquired only in the course of the ages. This power to stand and to walk in an upright position was acquired by slow stages in the old Lemurian Epoch, and we now recapitulate it in infancy before our Ego awakens to consciousness. This pre-knowledge is crowded into a time of life when the process does not yet depend upon our consciousness but works as an unconscious impulse towards the upright position."

"Man, in the early stages of his life and before his Ego-consciousness has awakened, is destined by means of the rudiments of this Ego to bring himself to a vertical position, to raise himself out of the condition he still occupied during the Old Moon period when the line of direction of his spine was practically horizontal, parallel with the Moon's surface. During the old Lemurian time he learnt to alter the Old Moon direction to that of the Earth. This came about because, during the Earth development, the Spirits of Form poured the Ego into man out of their own substance. And the first manifestation of this in-flowing of the 'I' was that inner force by means of which man raised himself into an upright position. Thus, through this position, he is wrested from the Earth. The Earth contains within itself spiritual forces capable of streaming through the spine as in the case of the animal body where in its natural growth it remains horizontal. But the Earth has no forces enabling it directly to serve the human being who, through his Ego when it awakens later to consciousness, can raise himself upright. In order that man may develop harmoniously with an upright position and vertical walk, forces had to stream into the Earth from the Cosmos, the extra-earthly. If, during the old Lemurian Epoch, the first Christ-event had not taken place, Lucifer and Ahriman would have been able to bring about disaster to the whole of humanity since man, through his upright position, was wrested from the spiritual forces of the Earth. In that old Lemurian Epoch, in the realm which is the nearest spiritual sphere to our Earth, the Being—at that time, however, of an Angelic nature—who later on became the Nathan-Jesus, was permeated with the Christ-Being."

"This was the first stage of the Mystery of Golgotha. The consequence was that in that old Lemurian Epoch—but in etheric spiritual heights—the being who later became the Nathan-Jesus, and who otherwise would have had the form of an Angel, took on human form (not of flesh, but a human etheric form). In the super-earthly region Jesus of Nazareth is to be found as an etheric Angel form. Through permeation with the Christ, he then assumed etheric human form. Thereby something new entered the Cosmos and rayed down upon Earth and made it possible for man, the physical earthly human form, into whom streamed the force of the etheric super-earthly Christ-Being, to protect himself from that destruction which must have overtaken him had not the Formative Force, which enabled him to become an upright harmonious being, permeated and lived on in him. Disorder must inevitably have entered had not this form-giving force, which was able to stream into mankind because of the first Christ-event, poured in with the forces of the physical Sun. This which man received into himself in the old Lemurian Epoch has since lived on in the evolution of humanity. We take the right view of a growing child when we see him emerging from the crawling, wriggling, helpless state and managing for the first time to stand upright or walk, when we realize that his being able to do so has only become possible because the first Christ-event took place in the old Lemurian time for the help and salvation or mankind; because he who, as the Nathan-Jesus, was permeated by Christ, took on as a spiritual etheric being the human etheric form as the result of that permeation."

"Yes, my dear friends, Spiritual Science is here that we may enrich our feelings. Such a feeling as can live in our souls when we see a little child learning to stand upright and to walk has most certainly a deep religious background. We should often call to mind why the child walks and realize how we must thank the Christ-impulse for it. Then we have enriched our conception of the world through Spiritual Science and acquired a feeling for our environment which we could not possess otherwise. Through Spiritual Science we take note, as it were, of the protectors and guardians of a child's growth and development and see how the Christ-Force radiates around his being."

"The Atlantean man was actually the first to learn to speak, and the Akashic Records show how that came about. Learning to speak is the second capacity which a child acquires before the actual Ego-consciousness awakens, the awakening coming after he has learnt to speak. Learning to speak depends altogether on a kind of imitation, the aptitude for which, however, is deeply embedded in human nature. Speech came to man as a consequence of progressive development. The Spirits of Form poured themselves into man and permeated him, and thereby he became able to speak a language, to live his earth life on the physical plane."

"Thus, by means of two principles, viz., the upright position and speech, he wrests himself free from those spiritual forces that are active upon the Earth. Man has made himself independent of those forces which spiritually flow through the Earth, just as through acquiring the power to stand upright he made himself independent of the first stream. If he had been abandoned entirely to the Earth, if Cosmic-spiritual influences had not come down to Earth and poured into him, everything connected with his speech must have become debased through the Luciferic and Ahrimanic influences. If nothing had been brought about by Christ, man in the Atlantean Epoch would so have developed his whole life-culture—all his bodily organs: larynx, tongue, throat, etc., and indeed even the organs lower down such as the heart in so far as they are connected with the former—that he would only have been capable of expressing his own selfish joy or pain, desire or bliss, in poor babbling sounds somewhat like the utterances of Sibyls or mediums. Certainly, he would have been able to utter much more artistic or intelligent sounds than an animal can produce, but these sounds would only have been expressive of that which lived within him, of the bodily processes taking place in his organism. He would have found expressive interjections for these only; his speech would have consisted entirely of interjections. Whereas we now limit our interjections to a few words, the human art of speech with all its subtleties would have developed at that time only as far as a language of such interjections. This disorder in the power of speech in so far as it would have affected man's inner being was averted; the second Christ-event prevented it from entering human evolution. Through the fact that for the second time the Being in the etheric heights, who later became the Nathan-Jesus child, received into himself the Christ-being who henceforward permeated the bodily organs of man, man became capable of uttering more than interjections. The power of grasping the objective was brought about through the second Christ-event."

"But the human capacity for expressing the working of the mind in words was again faced with danger. Through the second Christ-event it might indeed have come to pass that man would have found not only sounds, interjections and words to express the feelings of his inner being; in a certain sense he might also have been able to give out what he had called forth as an inner speech movement. But the power of describing outer things in words, in order that the words should rightly indicate them, was still in danger from the luciferic and ahrimanic influences right into the Atlantean Epoch. Then came the third Christ-event. For the third time that Being in the spiritual heights, later to be born as the Nathan-Jesus, united himself with the Christ-being and again poured the forces so received into the human power of speech. The force of this Christ-Jesus Being now permeated once more the organs of the human body in so far as those organs come to expression in the power of speech. In this way it was made possible for the power of speech to create, by means of words, actual signs representative of the external environment, thus enabling mankind to create language as a means of communication between the different inhabited regions. A child learns to speak, but he could never do so if these two Christ-events had not taken place during the Atlantean Epoch. Through Spiritual Science we can enrich anew our inner feelings if we remember, when we see a child beginning to speak and gradually improving his power of expression, that the Christ-impulses rule within the unconscious nature and that the Christ-Force lives in the child's power of speech, guarding and stimulating it."

"After the occurrence of the three Christ-events, which have again been described today from a certain standpoint in their influence on human evolution, came the Post-Atlantean Epoch. In this evolution the mission of the peoples belonging chiefly to that stage of man's development known to us as the Egyptian-Chaldean Period [2907 BC-747 BC] was to recapitulate what had happened for humanity in the Lemurian Epoch; but at the same time to permeate it with consciousness. Quite unconsciously man learnt to stand upright in the Lemurian Epoch, and to become a speaking being in the Atlantean Epoch. Quite unconsciously he took in the Christ-impulse at that time because his power of thought had not been awakened. In the Post-Atlantean Epoch [7227 BC-7894 AD] he has had to be led slowly to understand what it was that he had thus taken in unconsciously in prehistoric ages. It was the Christ-impulse which enabled him to stand upright and look up into the cosmic heights. In the Lemurian Epoch man lived as he was obliged to do. Later the peoples of Egypt, who were not yet fully conscious but in a condition preparatory to the attainment of full consciousness, had to be led to revere what dwells in the human power of erectness. The Initiates, whose mission it was to influence the culture of Egypt, taught the people to revere that power by causing them to build the pyramids which reach up from the earth towards the Cosmos. Even now we cannot but marvel at the way in which, through the working of the cosmic forces into the whole form and position of these structures, this power of the upright is brought to expression. The Obelisks were erected so that man might begin to penetrate into the power of the perpendicular. The wonderful hieroglyphics in the pyramids and on the obelisks, which were intended to point to the Christ, awakened to consciousness the super-earthly forces of the Lemurian Epoch."

"As regards the power of speech, however, the Egyptians could not even acquire that dim comprehension which they had for the power which enables man to stand upright. Their souls had first to undergo the right schooling, so that in later times they might be able to understand the riddle—how the Christ lives in man's gift of speech. That riddle was to be received with the most sacred reverence by the maturing human soul. This was provided for in the most wonderful way by the Hierophants, the Initiates of the Egyptia civilization, when they erected the enigmatic Sphinx with its dumb, granite form which only produced sound under the influence of the Cosmos when the human beings of that day were in an exalted state of consciousness. In the contemplation of the silent Sphinx, from which sound only proceeded at sunrise under certain cosmic conditions and in certain relations, there came to man that deep reverence by which the soul was prepared to understand the language which must be spoken when it would be brought to higher consciousness how the Christ-impulse gradually enters into the evolution of earthly humanity. That which the Sphinxes themselves could not yet say, although they prepared the way for it, had to be said to mankind. In the forming of the word-movement lies the Christ-impulse."

"A third thing which the child has to learn before he actually awakens to the Ego consciousness is to form ideas, to think. This power of thinking was reserved for the humanity of the Post-Atlantean Epoch; and, indeed, for the humanity of the fourth Period in that Epoch. Before that men thought in pictures. The child, too, thinks in pictures. It was only gradually given to humanity to think in thoughts, this faculty not being aroused in man until the sixth and seventh centuries before Christ. From that time onwards the thinking of thoughts has developed more and more; we now stand in the middle point. It is through the development of this power that the Ego can be grasped. In order that thinking, too, might be united with the Christ-impulse, that thinking as such might not come into disorder in its activity on the Ego, there came the fourth Christ-event, the Mystery of Golgotha."

"If our thinking is gradually to be brought more and more into order, to develop on the right lines so that our thoughts shall no longer be chaotic and confused, but filled, permeated with inner feeling, if there is to be an increasing development of healthy thinking based upon truth—it will be because thinking has acquired, through the Mystery of Golgotha, the fourth Christ-event, the impulse which it could only acquire as a result of the Christ-impulse having poured itself out into the spiritual atmosphere of the Earth. This outpouring occurred for the first time in the Lemurian Epoch when the upright position of man was threatened by Lucifer."

"It occurred for the second time in the Atlantean Epoch when man's power of speech which, as an expression of his inner being, was in danger of being disordered, was saved. Towards the end of the Atlantean Epoch it occurred for the third time. When the Christ permeated the spiritual being of the later Jesus of Nazareth, the gift of speech, inasmuch as words are signs which represent things in the outer world, was delivered by Christ from danger."

"The fourth danger was to man's thinking, the inner representation of his ideas. From this danger man is saved by permeation with thoughts on such forms as live within him—forms such as that which flowed out into the spiritual sphere of the Earth through the Mystery of Golgotha. This can be the case even now if man will prepare himself for it through Spiritual Science."

"Later Periods are always being prepared for during those that precede them. And inasmuch as we stand within the Fifth Post-Atlantean Period [1414 AD-3574 AD], inasmuch as we foster

Spiritual Science and have continuously more to contribute to the understanding of living thought, of the thinking which is becoming clairvoyant—we have at the same time the Sixth Post-Atlantean Period [3574 AD-5734]."

"Just as the Christ-impulse now streams into the thoughts of life, so will it stream later into something which is indeed one of the qualities of the human soul but must not be confused with mere thinking. The child develops his capacities out of the unconscious. When he attains to Ego-consciousness he enters the sphere in which he can acquire, in which he must develop, all that can come to him from outside through the Christ Impulse. When the child has learnt to walk, when he has learnt to speak, and when with learning to think, he has begun to work through to the Ego, we can see how the conscious Christ-impulse, which entered through the Mystery of Golgotha, begins gradually to work upon him. At the present time there is something else among the powers of the human soul which is not yet able to take in the Christ-impulse. It is possible to introduce the Christ-impulse into the power of walking upright, and into speaking and thinking, these things are possible because of that which has been done for the civilization of mankind for centuries."

"We have now to prepare for the introduction of the Christ-impulse into a fourth element, a fourth human capacity, if we truly stand on the foundation of Spiritual Science. The soul-capacity into which the Christ-impulse cannot yet be directed, but into which we must prepare to direct it, is the human memory. For in addition to the walking and standing upright, the speaking and thinking, the Christ-force is now entering the memory. We can understand the Christ when He speaks to us through the

Gospels. But we are only now being prepared as human beings for His entrance also into the thoughts which live in us and which then, as remembered thoughts and ideas, live on further in us. And a time will come for humanity which is now being prepared but which will only be fulfilled in the Sixth Great Period of humanity when men will look back upon that which they have lived through and experienced, upon that which lives on within them a memory. They will be able to realize that Christ Himself is present in the power of Memory. He will be able to speak through every idea. And if we make concepts and ideas alive within us Christ will be united with our memories, with that which as our memory is so closely and intimately bound up with us."

"Man, looking back at his life, will realize that just as he can remember, just as the power of recollection lives within him, so in this recollection there also lives the Christ-impulse which has streamed into it. The path which is shown to man is to make the words, "Not I, but Christ in me," more and more true. And the way will be made smooth through the Christ-impulse gradually drawing into man's power of memory. The Christ-impulse is not yet within the memory. When it actually comes, when it lives not only in the understanding of man but is poured out over the whole length and breadth of his memories, he will not have to turn to external documents to learn history, for then his whole power of memory will be extended. Christ will live in this memory. And when Christ has entered into the power of Memory, when Christ lives in that power, man will know that until the Mystery of Golgotha Christ worked outside the Earth; that He prepared for and went through that Mystery, and that He works on further as an Impulse in history. Man will be able to survey this in the same way as he now perceives facts which live in his ordinary life as Memory. He will not be able inwardly to survey the earthly evolution of humanity otherwise than by seeing the Christ-impulse as the central point. The whole power of Memory will be penetrated, and at the same time strengthened, by the entrance into it of the Christ-impulse."

"We shall be able to say that Christ is in our inner soul-life. Many of us will feel it to be so if we learn to unite ourselves with the Christ-impulse, even as the human child learns to stand upright and to speak because he has united himself with the Christ-impulse. Looking upon our present faculty of memory as a preparatory stage, many of us also realize that it must fall into disorder in the future unless it has the will to allow itself to be permeated with the Christ-impulse. Should there be upon the Earth a state of materialism in which the Christ is denied, the power of Memory would fall into disorder. More and more people would appear whose memory was chaotic, who would become duller and duller in their dark Ego consciousness if memory were not to shine into this darkness of the Ego."

"Our power of Memory can only develop in the right way if the Christ-impulse is perceived aright. History will then be a living memory because a true understanding of events has entered the memory; human memory will understand the central point of world-evolution. A perceptive faculty will then arise in man and his ordinary memory, which at present is only directed to one life, will extend over former incarnations Memory at the present time is in a preparatory stage, but it will be endowed through the Christ. Whether we look without and see how as children we have developed as yet unconsciously, or through an intensive deepening of our soul forces look within to what remains in our memory as our inner being—everywhere we behold the living force and activity of the Christ-impulse."

"The Christ-event which is now approaching us—not in the physical but in the etheric and connected with the first kindling of the power of Memory, with the first kindling of the Christ-permeated Memory—will be such that Christ will approach man as an Angel-like Being. For this event we must prepare ourselves."

Christ and the Spiritual World: The Search for the Holy Grail, Rudolf Steiner, Lecture III, December 30, 1913, GA 149

"Let us recall what is described in *Occult Science*—how from the Lemurian Age onwards souls gradually came down from the other planets (with the exception of one principal human pair who had stayed on earth) and were incarnated in human bodies throughout Atlantean times. We must accordingly think of Earth-evolution as being such that the souls withdrew from the Earth's cosmic surroundings and at various points of time took up again their evolution on Earth. We know that before the Lemurian Age they had gone away to other planets. But we know also that the evolution of the Earth had been exposed to the attacks of Lucifer, and later to those of Ahriman. Thus, the souls of men had to enter into bodies wherein they were exposed in the course of human evolution to the attacks of both these spiritual Beings. If nothing further had come about—if, that is, the human souls had come down from planetary existence into evolution on Earth, there to encounter the Luciferic and Ahrimanic influences—then something else would have happened to them as they went through subsequent incarnations."

"First of all, when human beings came down from the planets into physical bodies, the development of their senses would have been exposed to a certain danger. We must not think it was a quite simple matter for these human souls to come down from their planetary abodes and assume bodies on Earth, and that after that everything went on normally. Because the Luciferic and Ahrimanic principles held sway in these bodies, they were not so organized as to enable human beings to pursue the course of evolution which in fact they did pursue. If these souls had simply gone on using the forces which governed the sense-organs of these bodies, they would have had to use their senses in a peculiar way—a way not really human."

"And so, because of the Luciferic and Ahrimanic influences, the souls descending from the planets would have found no bodies equipped with senses of the right kind. They would have been tormented by sympathy and antipathy; on seeing one color or another they would have been seized with bliss or repulsed with acute pain, all through their lives. That was how evolution was going; cosmic forces, especially those from the Sun, would have worked on the Earth in such a way as to give the senses this character. Any contemplation of the world, in a spirit of quiet wisdom, would have been ruled out. So, a change had to be brought about in the forces which flowed from the cosmic environment into the Earth and had built up the senses of man. In the spiritual world something had to happen so that these forces would not turn the senses into mere organs of sympathy and antipathy, for they would then have been under the sway of Lucifer and Ahriman."

"Hence the following took place. The Being of whom we have said that he had not chosen the path down from the planets to the Earth, but had remained behind, the Being who later appeared as the Nathan Jesus-child and who had dwelt from primal ages in the spiritual worlds—this Being resolved while still in the world of the higher Hierarchies to go through a development which would enable him to be permeated for a time by the Christ Being. Thus, we have to do not with a man but with a superhuman Being who lived in the spiritual world and as it were heard the distress of the human sense system crying out to the spiritual world for help, and in response to this cry made himself fitted to be permeated by the Christ."

"So it was that in the spiritual worlds the Being who later became the Nathan Jesus child was permeated by the Christ Being, and then brought about a change in the cosmic forces which were streaming in to build up the human senses. These senses were changed in such a way that instead of being mere organs of sympathy and antipathy, they became organs that human beings could use, and so could look with wisdom at all the nuances of sense-perception. Very differently would the cosmic forces have flowed into mankind if this event, far back in the Lemurian Age, had not taken place in the spiritual worlds. This Being who appeared as the Nathan Jesus-child was then still living in the Sun-sphere, and because he listened to the human cry of distress, he experienced something which made it possible for him to be permeated by the very Spirit of the Sun, so that the activity of the Sun was modified in such a way that the human sense organs, which derive essentially from solar activity, did not become organs of mere sympathy and antipathy."

"Here we touch upon a significant cosmic secret, and one which will enable us to understand much that happened later on. A certain order and harmony, imbued with wisdom, could now flow into the realm of the human senses, and evolution could go on normally for a while. The worst activity of Lucifer and Ahriman had been turned away from the human senses by a deed in the higher worlds."

"Later on came a time, in the Atlantean Epoch, when it once more became apparent that the human bodily constitution could not be a suitable instrument for the further course of evolution. The human vital organs, and their underlying forces in the etheric body, which for a time had developed in a suitably useful way, had fallen into disorder. For the cosmic forces which had worked on them from the surroundings of the Earth, and whose task it was to bring order into these organs—the organs of breathing, blood circulation and so on—these forces would have developed under the influence of Lucifer and Ahriman in such a way that the vital organs would have ceased to be usable by human beings on Earth. They would have acquired a quite peculiar character. The forces which provide for these vital organs do not flow in directly from the Sun, but from the seven planets, as they used to be called. The planetary forces worked from the Cosmos into man. And it was necessary that these forces, also, should be modified. If they had remained under the sway of Lucifer and Ahriman, the vital organs would have become merely organs of greed or organs of loathing."

"So again, something had to happen in the spiritual worlds in order that this destructive activity should not enter into human life. And this same Being, who later appeared as the Nathan Jesus-child and who dwelt in earlier times on the Sun and was there permeated by the Christ Being, the sublime Sun-Spirit—this Being went from planet to planet, touched in his innermost nature by the fact that human evolution could go no further, as things were. And this experience affected him so strongly, while he was assuming a form of body on the different planets, that at a certain time during the Atlantean evolution the Spirit of Christ permeated him again. And through what was now brought about by the permeation of this Being by the Christ Spirit, it became possible for moderation to be implanted in the vital organs of man. In the same way that wisdom had been given to the sense-organs, so moderation was now bestowed on the vital organs. Thus, it came about that when a man breathed in a particular place, he was not impelled to suck in the air greedily, or to recoil with loathing from the air in another place. That was the deed accomplished in the spiritual worlds through a further permeation of the Nathan Jesus child by the Christ Being, the high Sun-Spirit."

"Then in the further course of human evolution a third thing happened. A third confusion would have arisen if the souls had been obliged to continue using the bodies then available for them on Earth. We can put it in the following way. At this time the physical nature of man was in order. Through the two Christ deeds in the super-sensible world, the human sense organs were in a condition serviceable for man on Earth, and so were the vital organs. But it was not so with the soul-organs, thinking, feeling, and willing. If nothing further had happened, these soul-organs would have become disordered. I mean that willing would have been continually disturbed by thinking, feeling would have interfered with willing, and so on. Men would have been condemned as it were to a perpetually chaotic use of these soul organs. This was the third great danger to which humanity was exposed on Earth."

"Now these three soul-powers, thinking, feeling, and willing, are coordinated from the surroundings of the Earth, for the Earth itself is essentially the scene of action for the Ego. The working together of thinking, feeling and willing has to be kept in order; not, however, from all the planets, but only from Sun, Moon and Earth, so that through the inter-working of Sun, Moon and Earth, if this is harmonious, man is made fit for the harmonious cooperation of his three soul-powers. Help for these soul-forces had to be provided from the spiritual world. And now the soul of that Being who later became the Nathan Jesus-child assumed a cosmic form such that his life was in a sense neither on the Moon nor on the Sun, but as though it encircled the Earth and felt a dependence on the influences of Sun, Moon, and Earth at the same time. The Earth influences came to him from below, the Sun and Moon influences from above. Clairvoyant observation really sees this Being, in the springtime of his evolution—if I may use that phrase—in the same sphere as that in which the Moon goes round the Earth. Hence, I cannot say exactly that the Moon influence came to him from above, but rather that it came to him from the place where he was, this pre-earthly Jesus-Being. Again, there rose to him a cry of distress, a cry that told of what human thinking, feeling, and willing were on the way to becoming; and he sought to experience completely in his own inner being this tragedy of human evolution. Thereby he called to himself the high Sun-spirit, who now for the third time descended upon him, permeating him. So, in the cosmic height, beyond the Earth, there was a third permeation of this Nathan Jesus-child by the high Sun Spirit whom we call the Christ."

"Now I would wish to depict for you this third ensouling rather differently from the way in which I described the other two. For it had effects which worked on into later times; the Sun's activity continued to be influenced by the fact that in ancient Lemurian times the Being who afterwards became the Nathan Jesus-child had been permeated by the Christ Being. And the essential thing about the initiation of Zarathustra was that he perceived the activity of the Sun impregnated with this influence. In this way his teaching arose; his initiation had revealed to him—had projected into his soul—what had happened in primeval times."

"The third post-Atlantean Epoch, which we call the Egyptian-Chaldean Epoch, came about partly through the reflection in human souls, as a continuing human experience, of the activities that had originated from the permeation by the Sun-Spirit of the Nathan Jesus-Being while that Being was journeying round the planets. From this arose that science of planetary activities which comes before us in Chaldean astrology; people today have a very meagre conception of what it really was. Among the Egyptian-Chaldean peoples of the Epoch there developed also that star worship which is indeed known exoterically; it arose because the moderating of planetary influence was still making itself felt at that later time."

"Later still, in the fourth post-Atlantean Epoch, we can see in Hellenism a reflection of planetary spirits who had as it were come into existence because the Being who had been permeated by the Christ journeyed from planet to planet and on each planet became one or other of these spirits. On Jupiter he became the one whom the Greeks later called Zeus; on Mars, the one later called Ares; on Mercury, the one later called Hermes. In the Greek planetary gods, there was this later reflection of what Christ Jesus in the super-sensible worlds had made of the planetary beings who were imbued with the Luciferic and Ahrimanic principles. When a Greek looked up to his heaven of the gods, he came into touch with the adumbrations, the reflections, of the activity of Christ Jesus on the individual planets, together with much else that I have described."

"To this was added as a third event the reflection or adumbration of that which the Jesus Being, in the later post-Atlantean times, had experienced as a celestial Being in relation to Sun, Moon and Earth. If we are to characterize this, we can say: The Christ "ensouled" himself in an Angelic Being. We say of Christ that he embodied himself in Jesus of Nazareth, but we are speaking now of an event that took place in spiritual worlds: the Christ "ensouled" himself in an Angelic Being. And the effect was that human thinking, feeling and willing took an orderly course. This was an important event, coming early in the evolution of humanity: the development of human soul-powers was brought into good order. The two earlier Christ events had brought order rather into the bodily constitution of man on Earth: what then had had to happen in the celestial worlds for this third event to come about?"

"It will be easier to recognize this third event if we look for the reflection of it in Greek mythology. For just as the planetary spirits projected themselves into the figures of Zeus, Ares, Hermes, Venus or Aphrodite, Kronos and so on, so was this third cosmic event reflected not only in Greek mythology but in the mythologies of the most diverse peoples. We can understand how it was reflected if we allow ourselves to compare the reflected images with their sources; if, that is, we compare what happened in Greece with what first happened in the Cosmos."

"What was it that happened up there in the Cosmos? The need was to drive out something which would have raged chaotically in human souls; this had to be overcome. The Angelic Being who was permeated with the Christ had to accomplish the deed of vanquishing and driving out from the human soul that which had to be driven out if thinking, feeling and willing were to be harmonized. And so there arises the picture—let us bring it vividly before our souls—of an Angelic Being, dwelling still in the spiritual worlds, who later became the Nathan Jesus-child: he appears to us ensouled by the Christ and thereby rendered capable of special deeds—able to drive out from thinking, feeling and willing the element which would have raged within them as a dragon and brought them into chaos."

"A reminiscence of this is preserved in all the pictures of St. George vanquishing the Dragon which are found in the records of human culture. St. George and the Dragon reflect that celestial event when the Christ ensouled the Jesus-Being and enabled him to drive the Dragon out of the soul-nature of man. This was a significant deed, made possible only with the help of Christ in the Being of Jesus, at that time an Angelic Being. For this Angelic Being had actually to connect himself with the Dragon-nature; to take on as it were the form of the Dragon in order to hold off the Dragon from the soul of man. He had to work from within the Dragon, so that the Dragon was ennobled and brought out of chaos into a kind of harmony. The training, the taming of the Dragon—that is the further task of this Being. And so, it came about that the Dragon indeed remained active, but because there was poured into him the influence and power of the Being I have described, he became the bearer of many revelations which proved their worth to human civilizations throughout the course of post-Atlantean evolution. Instead of the chaos of the Dragon manifesting in maddened or bewildered men, the primal wisdom of the post-Atlantean time came forth. Christ Jesus used the Dragon's blood, as it were, so that with His help it could transfuse human blood and thereby make human beings the vehicles of divine wisdom."

"It is remarkable how for the Greek mind one particular divine figure emerged from the others. The Greeks, we know, reverenced a variety of gods. These gods were the reflections or projections of the Beings who originated from the journey round the planets of the Being, permeated by the Christ, who later became the Nathan Jesus-child. The Greeks saw them in such a way that when they looked out into cosmic spaces, when they looked up through the light ether, they rightly ascribed to the planet Jupiter—in an inward spiritual, not an external, sense—the origin of the Being they spoke of as Zeus. So, they spoke of Pallas Athene, of Artemis, of the various planetary gods who were the reflections of what we have spoken about. But from these pictures of the various figures of the gods there emerged one figure—the figure of Apollo."

"Because through the power of song and string-music he brings thinking, feeling and willing into harmony. We have only to keep firmly in mind that in Apollo there was a projection of what had happened at the end of the Atlantean time. Something had then worked from spiritual heights into the human soul, and a weak echo of it could be heard in the musical art cultivated by the Greeks under the protection of Apollo. They knew it as an earthly reflection of the ancient art which the Angel-Being, permeated by the Christ, had cultivated in the heavenly heights in order to bring thinking, feeling and willing into harmony."

"A celestial Being who from the higher worlds poured out healing forces for the soul, paralyzing the Luciferic and Ahrimanic powers. These forces brought about in the human body a harmonious co-operation of brain, breath and lungs with the larynx and the heart, and it was this that came to expression in song. For the right co-operation of brain and breathing with the speech organ and the heart is the bodily expression of harmony in thinking, feeling and willing. The Healer, the celestial Healer, is Apollo. We have seen this Being pass through three stages of evolution, and then the Healer, whom Apollo reflected, was born on Earth and men called him Jesus, which in our language means "He who heals through God". He is the Nathan Jesus-child, the one who heals through God, Jehoschua-Jesus."

"Now, at this fourth stage, this Being made himself ripe to be infilled with the Christ Being, with the 'I'. This came to pass through the Mystery of Golgotha. For if this Mystery had not been enacted—if the Being whom we have followed through cosmic ages had not given embodiment to the Christ—then in the course of later time human souls would not have found bodies in which the Ego-force could come to necessary expression on Earth. The Ego had been brought to its highest stage in Zarathustra. The souls who had taken part in the evolution of the Ego would never have found earthly bodies suitable for its further development if the Mystery of Golgotha had not come to pass."

"We have now seen the four stages of harmonization: the harmonizing of sense perception, of the life-organs, of thinking, feeling and willing, and the harmonization in the Ego, this last through the Mystery of Golgotha. You have the connections between the Being who was born as the Nathan Jesus-child and the Christ Being, and the way in which this was prepared."

Dr. Steiner has pointed out the way for deeper inner work in meditation on the unfoldment of the gifts of childhood. Out of active work and communion with these forces can we come to behold and understand what is meant by the following picture given by Dr. Steiner in the lecture series entitled, *The Spiritual Guidance of Man* (The Anthroposophic Press, Spring Valley, N.Y., 1950, p.17-18):

> "It was the deeds of the Christ which intervened and built the possibility of human Ego development through three specific Pre-Earthly Deeds and the culmination of creation in the Fourth Deed called the Mystery of Golgotha. The First Deed was accomplished during the Lemurian times in what has been subsequently called The Garden of Eden."

This First Pre-Earthly Deed of Christ, in Lemuria, created the capacity of man's upright posture and subsequently the ability to walk. The Second Pre-Earthly Deed of Christ was accomplished in Atlantean times when there was a type of 'Garden of Eden.' There, Christ's Pre-Earthly Deed created the selfless ordering of humanity's sense organs; or simply stated, the gift of speech in mankind. In the Atlantean Epoch, when the human being faced a distortion of the seven vital organs from the adversarial powers that would have made human organs selfishly fight against each other, there was a need for the Second Pre-Earthly

Deed of Christ. Working in the realm of the Elohim with the Nathan Jesus [Adam Kadmon], Christ sacrificed his etheric forces so that human language could be objective and able to channel creatively the "Word" of God in truth.

Again later in Atlantean times, the Third Pre-Earthly Deed of Christ selflessly ordered humanity's vital organs into a cooperative thinking, feeling and willing so that objective thinking could arise.

The Four Sacrifices of Christ, Rudolf Steiner, Basel, June 1, 1914, GA 152

"In our present civilization we need, above all, a new knowledge of Christ. In His three preparatory steps, taken before the actual Mystery of Golgotha, Christ provided for the complete evolution of humanity. The Being whom we acknowledge as the Christ clothed Himself once in a human body, in the body of Jesus of Nazareth. But this act was preceded by three preparatory steps. Three times earlier something of a similar nature occurred, not as yet on earth but in the spiritual world, and we have in a sense, three Mysteries of Golgotha that had not yet been fulfilled upon the physical plane. Only the fourth took place in the physical realm, as related in the *Gospels* and in the *Epistles of Paul*. This greatest of earthly events was prepared for by three supramundane acts, one taking place in the old Lemurian period and two in the Atlantean."

"While the earth was working through the Lemurian Age, a Being living in spiritual heights became manifest—one might say, as a sort of prophecy of John's baptism—in an Archangel who offered up his soul powers and was thus permeated by the Christ. Through this means a force was released that acted within human evolution upon earth. Its effect was a quieting and harmonizing of our senses so that today we can use them and find them selfless. If we, understanding this, have become grateful to the world order, we shall say, looking back to these ancient times, that what makes it possible for us as sensory beings to enjoy without pain all the splendor of surrounding nature is Christ's first sacrifice. By ensouling Himself in an Archangel He brought forth the power to avert the danger of the selfish senses in man. That was the first step leading to the Mystery of Golgotha."

"In the first period of the Atlantean evolution selfishness tried— this time through Lucifer and Ahriman—to take possession of another part of the human organism; that is, the vital organs. Had it depended upon Lucifer and Ahriman, quite a different state would have existed as early as the Atlantean period. Every single human organ would have been self-seeking, and the results most extraordinary. If we had become what Lucifer and Ahriman intended and had been thrown upon our own resources, we should have been chased about the world by animal desires for what satisfied one organ or another, or by terrible disgust for all that was injurious."

"That this did not happen, that our vital organs were subdued and harmonized resulted from the great event in the first Atlantean Epoch when, in supramundane spheres, the second step was taken toward the Mystery of Golgotha. The Christ Being ensouled Himself again in an Archangel, and what was accomplished by this deed shone down into the earth's atmosphere. Then that harmonizing and balancing of the vital organs took place that rendered them selfless."

"In our connection with the outer world, we should be continuously exposed to severe illnesses, and we could not be at all healthy but for this second Christ deed. In the last part of the Atlantean period humanity faced a third danger. Thinking, feeling, and willing were threatened with disorder through the entrance of selfishness. It was necessary for human evolution that thinking, feeling, and willing should become unselfish members of the united soul. Under the influence of Lucifer and Ahriman they could not have done this. Thought, feeling and will, becoming independently self-seeking, would have rent asunder the harmonious working of the Christ. In consequence, toward the end of the Atlantean evolution, the third Christ deed occurred."

"Once more the Christ Being ensouled Himself in an Archangel, and the power thus generated in the spiritual world made possible the harmonization of thinking, feeling, and willing. Truly, as the rays of the physical Sun must act upon Earth to prevent the withering of plant life, so must the Sun-Spirit be reflected upon Earth from supramundane spheres as I have just explained."

"What would have become of the human being without this third Christ event? As if by furies, he would have been seized by his unruly desires, by the activity of his will. He might have gone mad even though his self-seeking reason might have thought with scornful mockery about all that the raging will brought forth. This was averted by the third Christ deed when Christ took for the third time the soul of an Archangel as an outer vehicle."

"St. George who conquers the dragon, or Michael who conquers the dragon, are symbols of the third Christ event, when Christ ensouled Himself in an Archangel. It is the dragon, trodden under foot, that has brought thinking, feeling, and willing into disorder. So, the Sun Spirit became the guardian of the wild, stormy passions when they, as it sometimes happened, gushed forth in the fumes that rise from within the earth and break through its surface. For the Greeks, Apollo, the Sun Spirit, represented the Christ at the stage of His third sacrifice. In this connection Apollo was to the Greeks what is expressed in the victory of Michael or St. George over the dragon. Then came the fourth, the earthly mystery, that of Golgotha. The same Christ Being Who had ensouled Himself three times in Archangelic form incarnated through what we call the Baptism by John in the Jordan in the body of Jesus of Nazareth."

"Then came the fourth step in the Mystery of Golgotha, and this averted another danger, that of the luciferic and ahrimanic influences upon the human Ego or "I". In the Lemurian Age the sense organs would have become disordered through Lucifer; in the first Atlantean period the vital organs were threatened with disorder and disharmony, and in the late Atlantean era the soul organs, the organs that underlie thinking, feeling and willing. In the Post-Atlantean Period the human Ego itself was endangered."

"Standing in this space, is the Christ, incarnate in a human body, Who had to bring into order and harmony the Ego that was to come into the world. Yes, the science of the spirit will impress upon us ever more deeply that this human Ego, through the fourth Christ deed, the Mystery of Golgotha, can come to true unselfishness. The senses have said, "Not I, but Christ in us." The vital organs have said, "Not I, but Christ in us." In his moral and intellectual life man must learn to say, "Not I, but Christ in me." Every step into the spiritual world shows us this. The Christ-impulse will become for us the living bridge between earthly life and life in superphysical worlds. From the spiritual world Christ three times conditioned for the human being the spiritual constitution that he needed in order to live rightly. Christ intervened three times, making the human senses, life, and psychic organs unselfish. It is now man's task to learn unselfishness in his moral and intellectual life through his understanding of the saying, "Not I, but Christ in me."

"The world will recognize that the message of the science of the spirit is the Word of Christ. We can work up gradually to such a deep understanding of the Mystery of Golgotha as this by completely imbuing ourselves with Spiritual Science. If we thus consider this and, in addition, think of it as a school of unselfishness for the intellectual and moral life of future humanity, we shall realize the necessity of the spiritually scientific proclamation of the Mystery of Golgotha!"

Krishna—Christ's Pre-Earthly Deed in India

The Principle of Spiritual Economy, **Rudolf Steiner, Lecture VII,** *The Macrocosmic and the Microcosmic Fire*, **Cologne, April 10, 1909, GA 109**

"The religions could not teach what one might call the self-induced salvation of the human Ego as long as the Ego, whose physical expression is in the blood, was not touched by an impulse now present on earth. And thus, we are told how the great spiritual beings—the great avatars—descend and incarnate themselves from time to time in human bodies, especially when humanity needs help. These are beings who do not need to descend into a human body to enhance their own development because they have completed their own human development in an earlier cycle of the world. They descend for the sole purpose of helping human beings. For example, when mankind is in need of help, the great god Vishnu descends from time to time into an earthly existence. Krishna, one of the incarnations of Vishnu, speaks of himself and explains clearly what the essence of an avatar is. In the divine poem, the *Bhagavad Gita*, he himself explains what he is. Here we have the wonderful words that Krishna, in whom Vishnu lives as an avatar, says about himself: "I am the spirit of creation, its beginning, its middle, its end; I am the Sun among the stars, fire among the elements, the great ocean among the waters, the eternal snake among all snakes. I am the basis of everything."

"The Krishna-Being indwells in any human as the great ideal to which the human core strives to develop itself from within. And if, as the wisdom of antiquity endeavored to do, the human breath can be spiritualized through the impulse that we absorb through the Mystery of Golgotha, then we have realized the principle of salvation through that which itself lives within us. All avatars saved mankind through the forces they caused to radiate from spiritual heights down onto earth. The avatar Christ, however, saved mankind by means of what He Himself extracted from the strength of mankind, and He showed us how the strength to be saved and to conquer matter through spirit can be found within ourselves."

The Occult Significance of the Bhagavad Gita, **Rudolf Steiner, Lecture VII, Helsingfors, June 3, 1913, GA 146**

"When Arjuna stood on the battlefield with the Kurus and Pandus arrayed against each other, when he felt all that was going on around him and deeply realized the unique situation in which he was placed, it came about that this soul we have mentioned spoke to him through the soul of his charioteer. The manifestation of this special soul, speaking through a human soul, is none other than Krishna. For what soul was it that could instill into man the impulse to consciousness of self? It was the soul that had remained behind in the old Lemurian age when men entered his actual earthly evolution."

"This soul had often been visible in manifestations before, but in a far more spiritual form. At the moment, however, of which the *Bhagavad Gita* tells us, we have to imagine a kind of embodiment, though much concealed in Maya of this soul of Krishna. Later on in history, a definite incarnation takes place. This soul actually incarnated in the body of a child. Those of our friends to whom I have spoken of this before now that at the time when Christianity was founded two children were born in different families, both from the house of David. The one child is mentioned in the *Gospel of St. Matthew*, the other in St. Luke's. This is the true reason for the external discrepancies between the two Gospels. Now this very Jesus Child of *St. Luke's Gospel* is an incarnation of that same soul that had never before lived in a human body but is nevertheless a human soul, having been one in the ancient Lemurian Age. This is the same that revealed itself as Krishna. Thus, we have all that the Krishna impulse signifies incarnated in the body of the Luke Jesus child."

Lecture I

"We are told how, in the midst of the battle, Krishna appears and unveils before Arjuna cosmic secrets, great immense teachings. Then Krishna appears to him a form that embraces all things, a great, sublime, glorious beauty, a nobility that reveals cosmic mysteries. Krishna then is that being who has worked through centuries and centuries on the human organism, to make man capable—from the seventh and eighth centuries B.C. onward—of entering gradually the Epoch of self-consciousness. What kind of impression does he make, this master-builder of the human Ego-nature? He has to speak to Arjuna in words saturated through and through with self-consciousness."

Lecture V

"Thus, from another side we understand Krishna as the divine architect of what prepared and brought about self-consciousness in man. The Bhagavad Gita tells us how under special circumstances a man could come into the presence of this divine builder of his nature. There we have one aspect of Krishna's nature."

Lecture VI

"…Krishna spoke to Arjuna and poured into Arjuna's ears the most powerful, incisive, burning words to quicken the consciousness of self in man. In the whole range of the world's life there is nothing to be found that kindled the self of man more mightily than the living force of Krishna's words to Arjuna. The highest impulse that can speak to the individual man speaks through Krishna to Arjuna…"

"The highest to which the individual man can lift himself by raising to their full pitch all the powers that reside within his being—that is Krishna. The highest to which he can soar by training himself and working on himself with wisdom—that is Krishna…"

"…The Krishna Impulse comes into man's soul when from the depths of his own inner being he works, creates, and draws forth his powers more and more until he may rise into those realms where he may reach Krishna. But something came toward humanity from outside, which men could never have reached through the forces that lived within themselves; something bending down to each individual one… the Christ…"

"…If we look back to all that happened between the tenth century before Christ and the tenth century afterward, we may say that into the universe the Krishna Impulse flowed for every individual human soul, and into the earth the Christ-impulse came for all mankind."

Lecture VII

"We touch here upon a wonderful mystery. We see how into the body of the Luke Jesus child there enters the soul of man as he was before he descended into the course of earthly incarnations. We understand that this soul could hold sway in the human body only until the twelfth year of its life. After that another soul must take possession, the Zarathustra soul that had gone through all the transformations of mankind. This wonderful mystery is enacted that the innermost essence and self of man, which we have seen hailed as Krishna, permeates the Jesus child of the *Gospel of St. Luke*. In this child are the innermost forces of humanity, the Krishna forces, for indeed we know their origin. This Krishna root takes us back into the Lemurian Epoch, the very primeval age of man. At that time, it was one with humanity, before ever the physical evolution of mankind began. In later time this root, these Krishna forces, flowing together and uniting in the unknown and unseen, worked to bring about the unfolding of man's inner being from within. Concretely embodied, this root is present within a single being, the Luke Jesus child, and as the child grows up it remains active beneath the surface of life in this special body after the Zarathustra soul has entered it."

"In the thirtieth year, in the moment the *Bible* describes as the Baptism in Jordan, there comes toward this special human body what now belongs to all mankind. Christ now comes toward the physical body from the other side."

Lecture VIII

"In all that Krishna puts before Arjuna, when he presents himself as the founder of the age of self-consciousness, he has to speak in words altogether permeated by those shades of feeling derived from the concepts sattwa, rajas, and tamas. Thus is Krishna the great educator of the human Ego. He shows its separation from its environment. He explains soul activities according to how they partake of sattwa, rajas or tamas. Krishna, then, indicates to Arjuna how the different religious beliefs may be classified, and he also speaks to him of the different ways men may approach the Gods in actual prayer. In all cases the temper of man's soul can be described in terms of these three conditions."

Lecture IX

"The backbone of Krishna's teaching is how it directs man to put aside all externals, to become free from the life that takes its course in continually changing conditions of every kind; to comprehend oneself in the self alone, that it may be borne ever onward to higher perfection—asking how he shall perfect himself."

"Krishna—that is, the spirit who worked through Krishna—appeared again in the Jesus child of the Nathan line of the House of David, described in *St. Luke's Gospel*. Thus, fundamentally, this child embodied the impulse, all the forces that tend to make man independent and loosen him from external reality."

"In the personality of the St. Luke Jesus child Himself the Christ-impulse lived for three years; the Christ who came to mankind to bring together these two extremes. Through each of them mankind would have fallen into weakness and sin. Through Lucifer humanity would have been condemned to live one-sidedly in the external conditions of sattwa, rajas, and tamas. Through Krishna they were to be educated for the other extreme, to close their eyes and seek only their own perfection. Christ took the sin upon Himself. He gave to men what reconciles the two one-sided tendencies. He took upon Himself the sin of self-consciousness that would close its eyes to the world outside. He took upon Himself the sin of Krishna, and of all who would commit his sin, and He took upon Himself the sin of Lucifer and of all who would commit the sin of fixing their attention on externalities. By taking both extremes upon Himself he makes it possible for humanity by degrees to find a harmony between the inner and the outer world because in that harmony alone man's salvation is to be found."

"An evolution that has once begun, however, cannot end suddenly. The urge to self-consciousness that began with Krishna went on and on, increasing and intensifying self-consciousness more and more, bringing about estrangement from the outer world. In our time too this course is tending to continue. At the time when the Krishna impulse was received by the Luke Jesus child mankind was in the midst of this development, this increase of self-consciousness and estrangement from the outer world."

"The Christ-path must be added to the Jesus-path. To understand the Christ means not merely to strive toward perfection, but to receive in oneself something expressed by St. Paul, "Not I, but Christ in me." "I" is the Krishna word. "Not I, but Christ in me," is the Christian word. The two extremes—the Luciferic and the Krishna impulses—had to find their higher unity in the mission of the Christ."

The Bhagavad Gita and the Epistles of St. Paul, Rudolf Steiner, Lecture I, *The Uniform Plan of World History*, December 28, 1912, GA 142

"Just as Krishna made clear to his pupil that behind all existence is the creative cosmic Word, so also, he made clear to him that human knowledge can recognize the separate forms, and therefore can grasp the cosmic laws. The cosmic Word, the cosmic laws as echoed in the *Vedas*, and in Sankhya, were revealed by Krishna to his pupil. And he also spoke to him about the path that leads the individual pupil to the heights where he can once again share in the knowledge of the cosmic Word. Thus, Krishna also spoke of Yoga. Threefold is the teaching of Krishna: it teaches of the Word, of the Law, and of reverent devotion to the Spirit."

"Krishna teaches the highest human wisdom, the highest humanity, and he teaches it as being his own nature, and also in such a way that it is related to every human being, for all that is contained in the words of Krishna is to be found in germ in every human soul. Thus, when a man looks up to Krishna, he is both looking up to his own highest self and also at another: who can appear before him as another man in whom he honors that which he himself has the predisposition to become, yet who is a separate being from himself and bears the same relationship to him as a God does to man."

"Everything in the *Gita* refers to the great truths as to liberating oneself from works to the freeing of oneself from the immediate life of action, in order to devote oneself to contemplation, to the meditation of the soul, to the upward penetration of the soul into spiritual heights, to the purification of the soul; in short, according to the meaning of the *Gita*, to the union with Krishna."

"The Krishna-revelation is directed to one individual, but in reality applies to everyone if he is ripe to tread the upward path prescribed to him by the Lord of Yoga. The Christ-impulse, again, is something like a new group-soul of humanity, but one that must be consciously sought for by men. The object of human evolution, however, is that souls should become more and more differentiated."

"The spiritual path to Krishna can only be trodden by one who receives instructions from Krishna; the spiritual path to Christ can be trodden by anyone, for Christ brought the mystery for all men who feel drawn towards it."

"I have told you that there was, as it were, a sister-soul to the Adam-soul, to that soul which entered into the sequence of human generations. This sister-soul remained in the soul world. It was this sister-soul that was incarnated in the Luke-Jesus. But it was not then incarnated for the first time in a human body in the strictest sense of the words, it had already been once incarnated prophetically. This soul had already been made use of formerly as a messenger of the holy mysteries; it was, so to say, cherished and cultivated in the mysteries, and was sent whenever anything especially important to man was taking place; but it could only appear as a vision in the etheric body, and could only be perceived, strictly speaking, as long as the old clairvoyance remained. In earlier ages that still existed. Therefore, this old sister-soul of Adam had no need at that time to descend as far as the physical body in order to be seen. So, it actually appeared on Earth repeatedly in human evolution sent forth by the impulses of the mysteries, at all times when important things were to take place in the evolution of the Earth; but it did not require to incarnate, in ancient times, because clairvoyance was there. The first time it needed to incarnate was when the old clairvoyance was to be overcome through the transition of human evolution from the third to the Fourth Post-Atlantean Age, of which we spoke yesterday. Then, by way of compensation, it took on an incarnation, in order to be able to express itself at the time when clairvoyance no longer existed. The only time this sister-soul of Adam was compelled to appear and to become physically visible, it was incorporated, so to speak, in Krishna; and then it was incorporated again in the Luke-Jesus."

"So now we can understand how it was that Krishna spoke in such a superhuman manner, why he is the best teacher for the human Ego, why he represents, so to speak, a victory over the Ego, why he appears so psychically sublime. It is because he appears as human being at that sublime moment which we brought before our souls in the lecture before last, as Man not yet descended into human incarnations. He then appears again to be embodied in the Luke-Jesus. Hence that perfection that came about when the most significant world-conceptions of Asia, the Ego of Zarathustra and the spirit of Krishna, were united in the twelve-year-old Jesus described by St. Luke. He who spoke to the learned men in the Temple was therefore not only Zarathustra speaking as an Ego, but one who spoke from those sources from which Krishna at one time drew Yoga; he spoke of Yoga raised a stage higher; he united himself with the Krishna force, with Krishna himself, in order to continue to grow until his thirtieth year. Then only have we that complete, perfected body which could be taken possession of by the Christ."

"Thus do the spiritual currents of humanity flow together. So that in what happened at the Mystery of Golgotha, we really have a co-operation of the most important leaders of mankind, a synthesis of spirit-life. When St. Paul had his vision before Damascus, He Who appeared to him then was the Christ. The halo of light in which Christ was enveloped was Krishna. And because Christ has taken Krishna for His own soul-covering through which He then works on further, therefore in the light which shone there, in Christ Himself, there is all that was once upon a time contained in the sublime Gita. We find much of that old Krishna teaching, although scattered about, in the *New Testament* revelations. This old Krishna-teaching has on that account become a personal matter to the whole of mankind, because Christ is not as such a human Ego belonging to mankind, but to the Higher Hierarchies.

What one connects with Krishna can be compared with what, in more recent times, came to us in another philosophical form in the names of Fichte, Schelling and Hegel as the most mature thinkers of Christianity."

Incarnations of Lord Vishnu (Krishna) the Sustainer

The Ten Incarnations or Avatars of Lord Vishnu:

1. Matsya—a huge fish saved the life of Manu at the beginning of Satya Yuga.

2. Kurma—a giant tortoise carried the huge mountain Mandrachala used to churn the ocean.

3. Varaha—a wild boar who took the earth back to its original place.

4. Narasimha—a half lion and half human who killed the demon at dusk, with his nails, on the threshold of his house, keeping the demon on his thighs.

5. Vamana—incarnated as a Brahmin to end the rule of the demon-king, Bali.

6. Parashurama—incarnated as a Brahmin to end the tyrannical rule of unrighteous kings and unchaste women.

7. Lord Rama—appearing as King Rama he defeated demon-king Ravana after a fierce battle.

8. Lord Balarama—incarnated himself as Balarama, elder brother of Lord Krishna.

9. Lord Krishna—incarnated himself for two significant events—defeating his evil, maternal uncle and was the mentor of the Pandavas during the battle of Kurukshetra.

10. Kalki—will appear on a white horse with a mighty sword in our present age to destroy the evil existing in humanity.

***The Appearance of Christ in the Etheric, Spiritual Aspect of the Second Coming*, Sergei O. Prokofieff, Chapter I, *The Cosmic Dimension of Christ's Second Coming*, Temple Lodge: Forest Row, 2012, (pgs. 11-13)**

"For when a person turns consciously today to the spiritual world and forms a relationship to it in the pure mood of wonder and reverence, he will be helping the entelechy of Krishna-Jesus to enable the astral light-aura around the Christ to become ever stronger and more radiant. And if human beings offer up their selfless love to the spirit whom through Spiritual Science, they have recognized in all the beings and other entities around them, they can strengthen the etheric sheath that Vidar fashions today for the Christ. Moreover, through all deeds that they carry out today from their forces of conscience, which in the years to come will increasingly be transformed into the capacity to behold karma or destiny, people will be collaborating in the forming of the spiritual sphere around the Etheric Christ, which is the aim of Michael's activity today in the world bordering upon the Earth..."

"...Thus, one can see that, as people of our time, we lend strength to Christ's appearance in the etheric when, by developing within ourselves the three moral qualities that have been mentioned, we help the sister soul of Adam, Vidar, and Michael to form and strengthen the sheaths for the Etheric Christ. In this way, through our help and service we become the conscious collaborators of these spiritual beings in the Second Coming of Christ in the Etheric Realm, the most important supersensible event of our time."

Perfected Copies of Christ's Bodies

There is a wonderful source of ever renewing forces of life surrounding the Earth. It is called the super-etheric realm of the Earth, or Shambhala (Shamballa), New Jerusalem, or Eden Redeemed. This realm has been claimed by Sophia Christos as the redeemed part of the etheric already under Their control. Every perfected body of a saint, avatar, bodhisattva, or spiritual person is saved and imprinted for all time to come in this etheric sphere around the Earth. Once a perfected 'vehicle' is imprinted into this realm, it is available to copy itself for the use of any initiate who wishes to embody it and is deserving. This super-etheric realm is also called the Realm of Spiritual Economy where the spirit employs wise economy by replicating perfected bodies for those in like resonance.

The most profound aspect of the Realm of Spiritual Economy is that even the perfected bodies of Christ Jesus and Mary Sophia are imprinted in the super-etheric realm of Shamballa. St. Augustine, Johannes Tauler, Meister Ekhart, St. Francis, and Rudolf Steiner all used perfected vehicles from this realm. There is no need to create other perfected vehicles because the spirit knows how to utilize multi-dimensional holographic mirroring in the processes of creation and maintenance of the Universe. Humans who are emulating Christ, Sophia, saints, and great thinkers may use this realm of spiritual economy.

Christ joined His physical karma with the whole Earth and gave His life to re-enkindle of the forces of life that were waning. The Earth would have died and humanity would have failed in its evolution to become Angelic without Christ's interventions. Christ's blood and body went into the Earth and descended to its core. When Christ rose from the dead, He brought the renewed etheric and physical life of the Earth along with Him. After ascending to heaven, Christ is now bringing the dying etheric realm of the Earth and the human etheric body along with Him again in His continuing ascent.

The Principle of Spiritual Economy, From Buddha to Christ, Rudolf Steiner, Lecture XI, Budapest, May 31, 1909, GA 109

"We have already named three of the Masters: Zarathas, Skythianos, and Boddha or Buddha, and we can see how the lives of these leading personalities extend into our present time. An occultist can test these findings. In the realm of Spiritual Economy, we not only find what these exalted men left behind; everything else that is of value to humanity is preserved. In the Rosicrucian mysteries, too, we encounter the individuality who lived in the body of Buddha on the physical plane. During the Atlantean Age, he had lived only as a bodhisattva, but later on, he descended into the physical body of Buddha."

"The Christ was working in Buddha as a bodhisattva, and it was He who was now the planetary spirit of the earth since the event of Golgotha and who could since be found in the physical aura of the earth. Through the Christ-Principle a new light has been kindled in this world and beyond. The body of Jesus of Nazareth—the etheric and astral bodies and the Ego of Jesus of Nazareth—exist in many copies in the spiritual world. Many copies of the etheric and astral bodies and of the Ego of Jesus of Nazareth exist in order to be incorporated in the preliminary bearers of the Christ-principle. Everything connected with the

Christ-principle is so momentous that humanity can grasp it only little by little."

"St. Augustine, for example, bore within him a copy of the etheric body of Jesus of Nazareth. His Ego and his astral body were left to their own resources, and only in his etheric body did his great mystical gift come to life. St. Francis of Assisi and Thomas Aquinas had copies of the astral body of Jesus of Nazareth woven into their souls, and it is this fact that allowed them to be such dynamic teachers. Elisabeth of Thüringen also had an imprint of the astral body of Jesus of Nazareth in her soul."

"Zarathustra is one of the three Masters of the Rosicrucians. Many copies of his Ego, that is of the Ego in which the Christ Spirit Himself had dwelled, can be found in the spiritual world. The copies of the Ego of Jesus of Nazareth are waiting for us in the spiritual world to be utilized for the future evolution of humankind. People who endeavor to strive upward to the heights of spiritual wisdom and love are candidates for these copies of the Ego of Jesus of Nazareth. They become bearers of Christ. On this Earth they shall be heralds of His Second Coming."

The Principle of Spiritual Economy, Christianity in Human Evolution, Rudolf Steiner, Lecture II, Berlin, February 15, 1909, GA 109

"We have seen not only that the Egos are capable of reincarnation, but that the lower members of the human constitution in a certain sense undergo a similar process. The result of this is that the whole configuration of the process of reincarnation is much more complicated than is usually supposed. And thus, we see that the Ego of Zarathustra was reincarnated as Zarathas—Nazarathos, who in turn became the teacher of Pythagoras. On the other hand, Zarathustra's astral body reappeared in Hermes and his etheric body in Moses. Therefore, nothing is lost in the world; everything is preserved and transmitted to posterity, provided it is valuable enough."

"The etheric and astral bodies of Jesus of Nazareth were multiplied, and the copies preserved until they could be used in the course of human evolution. However, they were not bound up with this or that nationality or tribe. But when in the course of time a human being appeared who, irrespective of nationality, was mature and suitable enough to have his own etheric or astral body interwoven with a copy of the etheric or astral body of Jesus of Nazareth, then those bodies could be woven into that particular person's being. Thus, we see how it became possible in the course of time for all kinds of people to have copies of the astral or etheric body of Jesus of Nazareth woven into their souls."

"What made it possible for a number of people in those centuries to be able to receive revelations about the events in Palestine that were in a sense clairvoyant? It was possible because the multiplied copies of the etheric body of Jesus of Nazareth had been preserved and were in these centuries woven into the etheric bodies of a large number of people who wore these multiplied copies as one would wear a garment. Their etheric body did not consist entirely of the copy of Jesus' etheric body, but it had had woven into it a copy of the original. There were indeed human beings in those centuries who were able to have

Perfected Copies of Christ's Bodies   171

such an etheric body and who could thereby have an immediate knowledge of Jesus of Nazareth and the Christ."

"The highest degree of such disassociation is evident in that wonderful literary work of the ninth century, the Heliand. This poem was written down by a seemingly simple Saxon in the time of Louis the Pious, who reigned from 814-840. The Saxon's astral body and Ego could not match what was in his etheric body because the latter had had woven into it a copy of the etheric body of Jesus of Nazareth. This simple Saxon priest, the author of the poem, was certain from immediate clairvoyant vision that the Christ existed on the astral plane and that He was the same Christ who had been crucified at Golgotha! And because this was a direct certainty for him, he no longer needed to resort to historical documents or to physical mediation in order to know that the Christ does exist."

"If we continue to trace Christian development, we come to the period from about the eleventh or twelfth up to the fifteenth century, and it is here that we discover an entirely different mystery that now carried evolution forward. If you remember, first it was the memory of what had taken place on the physical plane, followed by the etheric element being woven into the etheric bodies of the pillars of Christianity in Central Europe. But later, from the twelfth to the fifteenth century, it was numerous copies of the astral body of Jesus of Nazareth that became interwoven with the astral bodies of the most important pillars of Christianity. In those days the human beings had Egos capable of forming extremely false ideas about all sorts of things, yet in their astral bodies a direct force of strength, of devotion, and of the immediate certainty of holy truths was alive. Such people possessed deep fervor, an absolutely direct conviction, and also in some circumstances the ability to prove this conviction. What sometimes must strike us as being so strange especially in these personalities is that their Ego development was not at all equal to that of their astral bodies because the latter had copies of the astral body of Jesus Christ woven into them. Their Ego behavior often seemed grotesque, but the world of their sentiments, feelings, and fervor was magnificent and exalted."

"Francis of Assisi, for example, was such a personality. We study his life and cannot, as modern people, understand what his conscious Ego was; yet we cannot help having the most profound reverence for the richness and range of his feelings and for all that he did. This is no longer a problem once we adopt the perspective mentioned above. He was one of those who had a copy of the astral body of Jesus of Nazareth woven into their own astral bodies, and this enabled him to accomplish what he did. Many of his followers in the Order of the Franciscans, with its servants and minorities, had such copies interwoven with their astral bodies in a similar fashion."

"…What was woven into Francis of Assisi was, as it were, the sentient soul of Jesus of Nazareth, and the same is true in the case of that remarkable personality Elisabeth of Thüringen, who was born in 1207. Knowing this secret of her life will enable you to follow the course of her life with your whole soul. She, too, was a personality who had a copy of the astral body of Jesus of Nazareth woven into her sentient soul. The riddle of the human being is solved for us by means of just such knowledge…"

"One may think of the content of scholasticism as one wishes, but for several centuries this school of thought developed the capacity of human reflection and thus put its imprint on the culture of the time. Scholasticism accomplished this by an extremely subtle discernment between and outlining of various concepts. As a result, between the thirteenth and fifteenth centuries the school implanted into humanity the capacity to think with acute and penetrating logic."

"The special conviction that Christ can be found in the human Ego arose among those who were imbued more strongly with the copy of the consciousness soul of Jesus of Nazareth, because the Ego functions in the consciousness soul. Because these individuals had within them the element of consciousness soul from the astral body of Jesus of Nazareth, the inner Christ rose resplendent within their souls, and through this astral body they came to know that the Christ within them was the Christ Himself. These were the individuals whom you know as Meister Eckhart, Johannes Tauler, and all other pillars of medieval mysticism."

Lecture III

"The mysteries of the Sun Oracle itself could not be directly revealed in ancient India, and that is why the seven Rishis spoke of a Being beyond their cognitive reach. They spoke of a Being who is the Leader of the Sun and directs its forces to the earth; they spoke of Vishva-Karman as a Being beyond the range of their knowledge. Vishva-Karman is none other than the Christ who was to appear later and who's coming had already been proclaimed in the ancient Indian culture."

"…In these early centuries, not all the inspired individuals destined to propagate the idea of Christianity were, of course, artists. Take, for example, John Scotus Erigena, the scholastic philosopher, who in the days of Charles the Bald wrote the famous *De Division Naturae*. He, too, had a copy of the etheric body of Jesus woven into his own etheric body."

"If human beings were born during the period from the fifth to the tenth centuries who had a copy of the etheric body of Jesus of Nazareth woven into their own etheric bodies, human beings living in the period from the eleventh to the fifteenth centuries received copies of the astral body of Jesus of Nazareth rather than copies of His etheric body. Only by considering this fact do we fully understand some of the important personalities of that time. How will a personality whose own astral body is interwoven with a copy of the astral body of Jesus appear to the outside world? After all, the Ego of Jesus is not incarnated in such an individual; each personality retains his or her own Ego. Ego judgment can cause many an error to creep into the life of such an individual; but because the copy of the great prototype has been woven into his or her astral body, devotion, all the feelings, everything in short that permeates and weaves through this astral body will come to the fore as the intrinsic essence of the astral body, even though it may perhaps be at variance with the Ego itself."

"Think of Francis of Assisi. There you have a personality into whose astral body a copy of the astral body of Jesus of Nazareth was woven. You may have found many extremes in the biography of Francis of Assisi, and if you did, you should consider that they were caused by his Ego, which was not on the same level with his astral body. But the moment you study his soul under the assumption that his Ego was not always capable of making the right judgments about the wonderful feelings and the humility contained in the astral body, then you will understand him. A copy of the astral body of Jesus of Nazareth was reincarnated in Francis of Assisi, and this was the case with many individuals of that time—Franciscans, Dominicans, and all other personalities of that time who will be intelligible only when studied in the light of this knowledge. For example, one of those personalities was the renowned St. Elisabeth of Thüringen."

"When Christ incarnated in Jesus of Nazareth, something like an imprint of the Ego was made in the astral body of Jesus of Nazareth. When the Christ Being entered the astral body, we can easily conceive that something like a replica of the Ego could be produced in the surrounding parts of the astral body. This copy of the Ego of Christ Jesus produced many duplicates that were preserved, so to speak, in the spiritual world. In the case of a few individuals who were to be prophets for their own age, something was woven into their Ego. Among them were the German mystics who proclaimed the inner Christ with such fervor because something like a copy of the Ego of Christ was incarnated in them—only a copy or image of Christ's Ego, of course. Only human beings who prepare themselves gradually for a full understanding of the Christ and who understand through their knowledge of the spiritual worlds what the Christ really is, as He surfaces time and again in ever changing forms during the course of human evolution—only those human beings will also gradually gain the maturity necessary to experience Christ in themselves. They will be ready to absorb, so to speak, the waiting replicas of the Christ-Ego, ready to absorb the Ego that the Christ imprinted in the body of Jesus."

"Part of the inner mission of the universal stream of spirituality is to prepare human beings to become so mature in soul that an ever-increasing number of them will be able to absorb a copy of the Ego-Being of Christ Jesus. For this is the course of Christian evolution: first, propagation on the physical plane, then through etheric bodies, and then through astral bodies that, by and large, were reincarnated astral bodies of Jesus. Now the time is at hand when the Ego-nature of Christ Jesus will increasingly light up in human beings as the innermost essence of their souls. Yes, these imprinted copies of the Christ Jesus individuality are waiting to be taken in by human souls—they are waiting!"

Lecture IV

"Immediately after the mystery of Golgotha when Christ's blood ran from five wounds and His spirit permeated the lowest realms, the incarnation of Christ brought about a remarkable change in the physical, etheric, and astral bodies of humanity. Christ's etheric and astral bodies multiplied like a grain of seed, and the spiritual world was filled with these copies. For example, human beings living in the period from the fifth or sixth through the tenth centuries who had developed sufficiently received at their birth such an imprint of the Christ-incarnation of Jesus of Nazareth."

"St. Augustine is the individual in whom such partaking in the etheric body of Christ is most clearly evident, and the great significance of his life must be attributed to this fact. On the other hand, Christ's astral body was incorporated into human beings from about the tenth to the sixteenth centuries, and this explains the appearance of human beings who were endowed with extraordinary humility and virtue, such as St. Francis of Assisi and the great Dominicans who reflected the wonderful astral qualities of Christ. These individuals were imbued with such a clear image of the great truths they practiced throughout their lives. By contrast, St. Augustine was never free of doubt and always experienced the conflict between theory and practice. Of the great Dominicans, St. Thomas Aquinas is especially noteworthy because in him the influence of the astral body of Christ was manifest to a high degree, as we shall see later. Beginning with the sixteenth century, copies of the Christ Ego begin to weave themselves into the Egos of a few individualities, one of them being Christian Rosenkreutz, the first Rosicrucian. This phenomenon led to the feasibility of a more intimate relationship with Christ, as is revealed by esoteric teaching."

"The power of Christ will make human beings more perfect, spiritualize them, and lead them back into the spiritual world. Mankind developed its reason at the expense of clairvoyance; the power of Christ will enable human beings to learn on this earth and to ascend again with what they will have acquired on earth. Human beings descended from the Father, and the power of Christ will lead them back to the Father."

Lecture VI

"When Christ descended to the earth, He enveloped Himself with the threefold physical, etheric, and astral bodies of Jesus of Nazareth and lived three years in this sheath as Christ, the Sun-Spirit. With the event of the Mystery of Golgotha, Christ descended to the earth; but aside from what is known to all of you, something else special happened by virtue of the fact that Christ indwelled the three bodies of Jesus of Nazareth, particularly the astral and etheric bodies. After Christ cast off the bodies of Jesus of Nazareth, they were still present as spiritual substance in the spiritual world but multiplied in a great many copies. They did not perish in the World Ether or in the astral world but continued to live as identical images. Just as the seed of a plant, once buried in the ground, reappears in many copies according to the mystery of number, so the copies of Jesus of Nazareth's etheric and astral bodies were present in the spiritual world. And for what purpose were they present, considering the large framework of spiritual economy? They were there to be preserved and to serve the overall progress of the human race."

"One of the first individuals to benefit from the blessed fact of these countless copies of Jesus's etheric body being present in the spiritual world was St. Augustine. When he again descended to earth after an earlier incarnation, not just any etheric body was woven into his own, but rather the copy of the etheric body of Jesus of Nazareth. Augustine had his own astral body and Ego, but his etheric body was interwoven with the image of the etheric body of Jesus. He had to work through the culture of his Ego and astral body, but when he had made his way to the etheric body, he realized the great truths that we find in his mystical writings."

"Many other human beings from the sixth to the ninth centuries had a copy of the etheric body of Jesus woven into their own etheric bodies. Many of these individuals conceived the Christian images that later were to be glorified in the arts in the form of the Madonna or the Christ on the cross. They were the creators of religious images who experienced in themselves what the people living at the time of the Mystery of Golgotha had experienced."

"In the period spanning the eleventh through the fifteenth centuries the time had come when a copy of the astral body of Jesus of Nazareth was woven into the astral bodies of certain reincarnated souls. From the eleventh to the fourteenth centuries many human beings, for example Francis of Assisi and Elisabeth of Thüringen, had the imprint of the astral body of Jesus of Nazareth woven into them while their own astral bodies—the source of their knowledge—were formed during reincarnation. This enabled these individuals to proclaim the great truths of Christianity in the form of judgments, logical constructs, and scientific wisdom. But, in addition, they were also able to experience the feeling of carrying the astral body of Jesus of Nazareth within themselves."

"Your eyes will be opened if you allow yourselves to experience vicariously all the humility, the devotion, and the Christian love that was part of Francis of Assisi. You will then know how to look at him as a person prone to make mistakes—because he possessed his own Ego—and as a great individual because he carried a copy of the astral body of Jesus of Nazareth within his own astral body. All the humble feelings, the profound mysticism, and the spiritual soul life of Francis of Assisi become comprehensible if we know this one secret of his life."

"Many other personalities in the world, such as Columban, Gallus, and Patrick, carried within themselves such a copy of Jesus's etheric body and were therefore in a position to spread Christianity and built a bridge from the Christ-event to the succeeding times."

"In the time from about the eleventh through the thirteenth centuries such human beings became the heralds of Christianity by the very fact that the astral body of Jesus was woven into their own astral body. Hence, they received Christianity by virtue of Grace. Although the Ego of Jesus of Nazareth left its three sheaths at the baptism of John, a copy of this Ego remained in each of them similar to the imprint a seal leaves behind. The Christ-being took possession of these three bodies and of that which remained as the imprint of the Jesus-Ego. Beginning with the twelfth, thirteenth, and fourteenth centuries, something like an Ego copy of Jesus was woven into human beings who began to speak of an "inner Christ." Meister Eckhart and Tauler were individuals who spoke from their own experience like an Ego copy of Jesus of Nazareth."

"There are still many people present who carry within themselves something like the various bodies of Jesus of Nazareth, but these are now no longer the leading personalities. Increasingly we can see how there are human beings in the Fifth Epoch who must rely on themselves and on their own Ego and how such inspired people have become a rarity. It was therefore necessary that a spiritual tendency develop in our Fifth Epoch to ensure that humanity would continue to be imbued with spiritual knowledge. Those individuals who were capable of looking into the future had to take care that human beings in the times to come would not be left simply to rely on their human Ego only. The legend of the Holy Grail relates that the chalice from which the Christ Jesus took the Last Supper with his disciples was kept in a certain place. We see in the story of Parsifal the course of a young person's education typical of our Fifth Post-Atlantean Epoch. Parsifal had been instructed not to ask too many questions, and his dilemma arose from his following those instructions."

"That is the important transition from the traditional to more modern times: in ancient India and later with Augustine and Francis of Assisi the student had to live in a state of the highest degree of passive devotion. All these humble people allowed themselves to be inspired by what was already alive in them and by what had been woven into them. But now things changed in that the Ego became a questioning Ego. Today, any soul that accepts passively what is given to it cannot transcend itself because it merely observes the happenings in the physical world around it. In our times, the soul has to ask questions; it has to rise above itself; it has to grow beyond its given form. It must raise questions, just as Parsifal ultimately learned to inquire after the mysteries of the Grail's Castle."

"Through this theosophical-Rosicrucian orientation of the spirit, we again bring close to ourselves what is still present in the copies of Jesus of Nazareth's Ego. Those who prepare themselves in this manner will pull into their souls the copy of the Ego of Jesus of Nazareth so that they become like imprints of a seal, and it is in this way that the Christ-principle finds its way into the human soul. Rosicrucianism prepared something positive, and since Anthroposophy is meant to become life, the souls that absorb and truly accept it will gradually undergo a metamorphosis. To accept Anthroposophy within yourself means to change the soul in such a way that it is able to come to a true understanding of the Christ."

Conclusion

The landscape of the etheric body of the human being is the domain that each person can make a difference in, for better or worse. Christ and the entire spiritual world stand ready to help each aspirant. But it is the free deed of the aspirant that either builds or destroys their personal etheric body. As for the etheric body of the Earth, suffice it to say, that battle is very visible and heated. The greedy are winning at this point and the Earth's life body has suffered great damage. Consciousness is being raised slowly to focus on sustainability and environmental homeostasis. The call to save Mother Earth has been heard and we will see who wins the battle. All of our lives are ultimately connected to that global battle. Inner and outer etheric awareness is crucial for the continuity of life on Earth.

As we behold Christ's activity in human evolution, we are struck with awe, reverence, wonder, and amazement. The intricate design of Christ's wisdom, manifesting through love, is wondrous to contemplate. Christ's divine deeds for humanity are miraculous and He continues His loving offerings in the etheric world to vouchsafe humanity's future. The knowledge of the Deeds of Christ enflames the initiate with spiritual resolve to accomplish loving, moral, conscientious deeds. Christ's great deeds are a type of spiritual nourishment that engender human spiritual deeds that reciprocally feed the divine world. The great Mystery of the Etheric Christ is the wonder of our age, and His Second Coming in the Etheric Realm is the salvation of human life.

Michaelic Verse For Our Times
by Rudolf Steiner

We must eradicate from the soul all fear and terror of
what comes toward us out of the future.
We must acquire serenity in all feelings and sensations about the future.
We must look forward with absolute equanimity to all that may come,
and we must think only that whatever comes is given to us
by a world direction full of wisdom.
This is what we have to learn in our times.
To live out of pure trust in the ever present help of the spiritual world.
Surely nothing else will do, if our courage is not to fail us.
Let us properly discipline our will, and let us seek
the inner awakening every morning and every evening.

BIBLIOGRAPHY

- Andreæ, Johann Valentin. *Reipublicæ Christianopolitanæ descriptio*. Argentorati: Sumptibus hæredum Lazari Zetzneri, Strasbourg, 1619.

- Andreæ, Johann Valentin. *Johann Valentin Andreae's Christianopolis; an ideal state of the seventeenth century*. translated from the Latin of Johann Valentin Andreae with an historical introduction. by Felix Emil Held. The Graduate School of the University of Illinois, Urbana- Champaign, 1916.

- Arnold, Edwin Sir. *The Light of Asia, or The Great Renunciation (Mahâbhinishkramana): Being the Life and Teaching Gautama, Prince of India and Founder of Buddhism (As Told in Verse by an Indian Buddhist)*. Kegan Paul, Trench, Trübner & Co., London, 1879.

- Avari, Burjor. *India: The Ancient Past: A History of the Indian Sub-Continent*. Routledge, New Edition, 2007.

- Barnwell, John. *The Arcana of the Grail Angel: The Spiritual Science of the Holy Blood and of the Holy Grail*. Verticordia Press, Bloomfield Hills, 1999.

- Barnwell, John. *The Arcana of Light on the Path: The Star Wisdom of the Tarot and Light on the Path*. Verticordia Press, Bloomfield Hills, 1999.

- Blavatsky, H. P. (Helena Petrovna). *Isis Unveiled: A Master-Key to the Mysteries of Ancient and Modern Science and Theology*. J. W. Bouton. New York, 1878.

- Blavatsky, H. P. (Helena Petrovna). *The Key to Theosophy: Being a Clear Exposition, in the Form of Question and Answer, of the Ethics, Science and Philosophy for the Study of Which the Theosophical Society Has Been Founded.* The Theosophical Publishing Company, Ltd. London, 1889.

- Blavatsky, H. P. (Helena Petrovna). *The Secret Doctrine: The Synthesis of Science, Religion and Philosophy.* The Theosophical Publishing Company, Ltd. London, 1888.

- Blavatsky, H. P. (Helena Petrovna). *The Voice of Silence: Being Extracts from the Book of the Golden Precepts.* Theosophical University Press, 1992.

- Bockemuhl, Jochen. *Toward a Phenomenology of the Etheric World: Investigations into the Life of Nature and Man.* Anthroposophic Press, Spring Valley, N. Y., 1977.

- Campanella, Tommaso. *The City of the Sun.* The ProjectGutenberg Ebook, David Widger, 2013.

- Colum, Padriac. *Orpheus: Myths of the World.* Floris Books. Colum, Padriac. The Children's Homer. MacMillan Co., 1946.

- Colum, Padriac. *The Tales of Ancient Egypt.* Henry Walck Incorporated, New York,1968.

- Crawford, John Martin. *The Kalevala: The Epic Poem of Finland.* John B. Alden, New York, 1888.

- Gabriel, Douglas. *The Eternal Curriculum for Wisdom Children: Intuitive Learning and the Etheric Body.* Our Spirit, Northville, 2017.

- Gabriel, Tyla. T*he Gospel of Sophia: The Biographies of the Divine Feminine Trinity*, Volume, Our Spirit, Northville, 2014.

- Gabriel, Tyla. *The Gospel of Sophia: A Modern Path of Initiation*, Volume 2. Our Spirit, Northville, 2015.

- Gabriel, Tyla and Douglas. *The Gospel of Sophia: Sophia Christos Initiation*, Volume 3. Our Spirit, Northville, 2016.

- Gabriel, Douglas. *The Spirit of Childhood*. Trinosophia Press, Berkley, 1993.

- Gabriel, Douglas. *The Eternal Ethers: A Theory of Everything*. Our Spirit, Northville, 2018.

- Gabriel, Douglas. *Goddess Meditations*. Trinosophia Press, Berkley, 1994.

- Gebser, Jean. *The Ever Present Origin*. Ohio University Press, 1991.

- Green, Roger Lancelyn & Heather Copley. *Tales of Ancient Egypt*. Puffin Books, New York, 1980.

- Harrison, C. G. *The Transcendental Universe; Six Lectures on Occult Science, Theosophy, and the Catholic Faith*. George Redway, London 1893.

- Harrison, C. G. *The Transcendental Universe; Six Lectures on Occult Science, Theosophy, and the Catholic Faith*. Delivered Before the Berean Society, edited with an introduction by Christopher Bamford. Lindesfarne Press, Hudson, 1993.

- Hamilton, Edith. *Mythology*. Little Brown And Co., Boston, 1942.

- Harrer, Dorothy. *Chapters from Ancient History*. Waldorf Publications, Chatham, 2016.

- Hazeltine, Alice Isabel. *Hero Tales from Many Lands*. Abingdon Press, New York, 1961.

- Heidel, Alexander. *The Babylonian Genesis: The Story of Creation.* University of Chicago Press, Chicago, 1942.

- Hiebel, Frederick. *The Gospel of Hellas.* Anthroposophic Press, New York, 1949.

- Jocelyn, Beredene. *Citizens of the Cosmos: Life's Unfolding from Conception through Death to Rebirth.* Continuum, New York, 1981.

- König, Karl. *Earth and Man.* Bio-Dynamic Literature, Wyoming, Rhode Island, 1982.

- Kovacs, Charles. *Ancient Mythologies and History.* Resource Books, Scotland, 1991.

- Kovacs, Charles. *Greek Mythology and History.* Resource Books, Scotland, 1991.

- Landscheidt, Theodor. *Sun-Earth-Man a Mesh of Cosmic Oscillations: How Planets Regulate Solar Eruptions, Geomagnetic Storms, Conditions of Life, and Economic Cycles.* Urania Trust, London, 1989.

- Laszlo, Ervin and Kingsley, Dennis L. *Dawn of the Akashic Age: New Consciousness, Quantum Resonance, and the Future of the World.* Inner Traditions, Rochester Vermont, 2013

- Plato. *The Republic.* Dover Thrift Editions, 2000.

- Sister Nivedita (Margaret E. Noble) & Coomaraswamy, Ananda K.. *Myths of the Hindus and Buddhists.* Henry Holt, New York 1914.

- Steiner, Rudolf. *Ancient Myths: Their Meaning and Connection with Evolution.* Steiner Book Center, 1971.

- Steiner, Rudolf. *Christ and the Spiritual World: The Search for the Holy Grail.* Rudolf Steiner Press, London, 1963.

- Steiner, Rudolf. *Foundations of Esotericism*. Rudolf Steiner Press, London, 1983.

- Steiner, Rudolf. *Isis Mary Sophia: Her Mission and Ours*. Steiner Books, 2003.

- Steiner, Rudolf. *Man as a Being of Sense and Perception*. Steiner Book Center, Vancouver, 1981.

- Steiner, Rudolf. *Man as Symphony of the Creative Word*. Rudolf Steiner Publishing, London, 1978.

- Steiner, Rudolf. *Occult Science*. Anthroposophic Press, NY, 1972.

- Steiner, Rudolf. *Rosicrucian Esotericism*. Anthroposophic Press, NY, 1978.

- Steiner, Rudolf. *Rosicrucian Wisdom: An Introduction*. Rudolf Steiner Press, London, 2000. GA 425

- Steiner, Rudolf. *The Bridge between Universal Spirituality and the Physical Constitution of Man*. Anthroposophic Press, NY, 1958.

- Steiner, Rudolf. *The Evolution of Consciousness*. Rudolf Steiner Press, London, 1926.

- Steiner, Rudolf. *The Goddess from Natura to the Divine Sophia*. Sophia Books, 2001.

- Steiner, Rudolf. *The Holy Grail: from the Works of Rudolf Steiner*. Compiled by Steven Roboz. Steiner Book Center, North Vancouver, 1984.

- Steiner, Rudolf. *The Influence of Spiritual Beings Upon Man*. Anthroposophic Press, NY, 1971.

- Steiner, Rudolf. *The Reappearance of Christ in the Etheric*. Anthroposophic Press, NY, 1983.

- Steiner, Rudolf. *The Risen Christ and the Etheric Christ*. Rudolf Steiner Press, London, 1969.

- Steiner, Rudolf. *The Search for the New Isis the Divine Sophia*. Mercury Press, N.Y., 1983.

- Steiner, Rudolf. *The Spiritual Hierarchies and the Physical World*. Anthroposophic Press, N.Y., 1996.

- Steiner, Rudolf. *The Tree of Life and the Tree of Knowledge*. Mercury Press, NY, 2006.

- Steiner, Rudolf. *The True Nature of the Second Coming*. Rudolf Steiner Press, London, 1971.

- Steiner, Rudolf. *Theosophy*. Anthroposophic Press. New York, 1986.

- Steiner, Rudolf. *Wonders of the World, Ordeals of the Soul, Revelations of the Spirit*. Rudolf Steiner Press, London, 1963.

- Steiner, Rudolf. *World History in Light of Anthroposophy*. Rudolf Steiner Press, London, 1977.

- Tappan, Eva March. *The Story of the Greek People*. Houghton Mifflin Co., Boston 1908.

- van Bemmelen, D. J. *Zarathustra: The First Prophet of Christ*, 2 Vols. Uitgeverij Vrij Geestesleven, The Netherlands, 1968.

- Watson, Jane Werner (Vālmīki). *Rama of the Golden Age: An Epic of India*. Garrard Pub., Champaign.

DIAGRAMS

Diagram I

The End of Kali Yuga and the Appearance of the Etheric Christ

The Kali Yuga (Sanskrit: n., कलियुग kaliyuga "age of Kali"

The 5,000 year Kali Yuga, the dark age,
is the last of the four Yugas,
the beginning of which Rudolf Steiner indicates as
the year c. 3,101 B.C. According to H. P. Blavatsky, and
Hindu Tradition, Kali Yuga began Feb. 18th, 3,102 B.C.
with the death of Krishna; as there is no year zero.

"...Kali Yuga began approximately in the year 3,101 B.C.
Thus we realize that our souls have appeared repeatedly
on the Earth in new incarnations,
in the course of which man's vision
has been more and more
shut off from the spiritual world
and therefore increasingly restricted
to the outer world of the senses..."
"...This was also the epoch of
John the Baptist,
of Christ Himself on Earth....
when 3,100 years of the
Dark Age had
already elapsed..." 1

Death of Krishna c. 3,101 B.C.

End of Kali Yuga 1,899 A.D.

The Mystery of Golgotha
33 A.D.

1 Rudolf Steiner, True Nature of the Second Coming,
I. The Event of Christ's Appearance in the Etheric World,
Karlsruhe July 25th, 1910 GA 118

Diagram II

The Resurrected Sophia and the Appearance of the Etheric Christ

Meeting with the being Anthroposophia

I. Quest for the Sophia
(Study of Spiritual Science)

II. Resurrection of the Sophia

Unconscious power of Christ within man

Living and conscious relationship with Christ
(experience of the Etheric Christ)

"We do not lack Christ; but the knowledge of Christ, the Sophia of Christ, the Isis of Christ is lacking. This is what we should engrave in our souls as a content of the mystery of Christmas." Rudolf Steiner

Diagram Source: "The Heavenly Sophia and the Being Anthroposophia," by Sergei O. Prokofieff, Temple Lodge: London, 1996

Diagram III

The Maitreya Buddha

"In fact the time is exactly determined when the successor of Gautama Buddha, Maitreya, will become a Buddha: five thousand years after the enlightenment of Buddha beneath the bodhi tree. Roughly three thousand years after our time the world will experience the Maitreya Buddha incarnation, which will be the last incarnation of Jeshu ben Pandira." 1

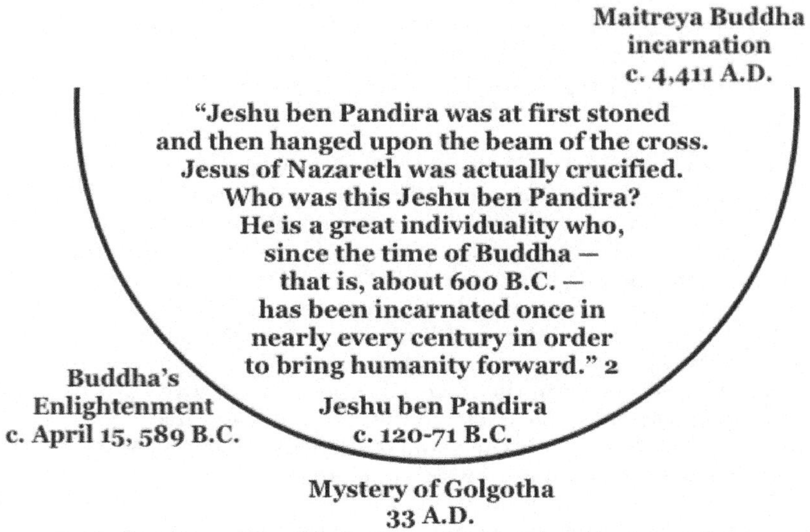

Maitreya Buddha
incarnation
c. 4,411 A.D.

"Jeshu ben Pandira was at first stoned and then hanged upon the beam of the cross. Jesus of Nazareth was actually crucified. Who was this Jeshu ben Pandira? He is a great individuality who, since the time of Buddha — that is, about 600 B.C. — has been incarnated once in nearly every century in order to bring humanity forward." 2

Buddha's
Enlightenment
c. April 15, 589 B.C.

Jeshu ben Pandira
c. 120-71 B.C.

Mystery of Golgotha
33 A.D.

1 Rudolf Steiner, The Christ Impulse in Historical Development I
Sep. 17, 1911 (GA 130)

2 Rudolf Steiner, Jeshu ben Pandira, Nov. 4, 1911 (GA 130)

Diagram IV

The Names of the Days of the Week and Human Evolution

Saturday = Saturn day
Sunday = Sun day
Monday = Moon day
Tuesday = Mardi = Mars day
(Týr being the Germanic Ares/Mars or god of war)
Wednesday = Mercury day = mercredi = Woden's day
(Woden/Wotan being the German Mercury)
Thursday = Jupiter day
Jupiter day = jeudi = Thor's day
(Thor being the Germanic Jupiter)
Friday = Venus day
Venus day = vendredi = Frig's day
(Frig being the Norse Venus)

The seven-fold evolution of our planetary system is reflected in the seven days of the week. We only need to be clear in our minds that esoterically the Earth is replaced by the two planets Mars and Mercury. The first half of Earth evolution, from the beginning to the middle of the Atlantean period relates to Mars, the second half to Mercury. While the Atlantean is deemed the 'middle,' as it is the 4th Epoch; due to the evolutionary process being retarded, the actual transition occurred in the Post-Atlantean Epoch, the 5th Epoch, through the incarnation of Christ at the "Turning Point of Time" which is the actual transition from the Mars half to the Mercury half of Earth evolution.

"Vulcan day was not established, as this is a recapitulation, just as an octave is a recapitulation of the tonic."
Rudolf Steiner in a letter to Marie von Sivers Nov. 25 1905

ABOUT DR. RUDOLF STEINER

Rudolf Steiner was born on the 27th of February 1861 in Kraljevec in the former Kingdom of Hungary and now Croatia. He studied at the College of Technology in Vienna and obtained his doctorate at the University of Rostock with a dissertation on Theory of Knowledge which concluded with the sentence: "The most important problem of human thinking is this: to understand the human being as a free personality, whose very foundation is himself."

He exchanged views widely with the personalities involved in cultural life and arts of his time. However, unlike them, he experienced the spiritual realm as the other side of reality. He gained access through exploration of consciousness using the same method as the natural scientist uses for the visible world in his external research. This widened perspective enabled him to give significant impulses in many areas such as art, pedagogy, curative education, medicine, agriculture, architecture, economics, and social sciences, aiming towards the spiritual renewal of civilization.

He gave his movement the name of "Anthroposophy" (the wisdom of humanity) after separating from the German section of the Theosophical Society, where he had acted as a general secretary. He then founded the Anthroposophical Society in 1913 which formed its center with the construction of the First Goetheanum in Dornach, Switzerland. Rudolf Steiner died on 30th March 1925 in Dornach. His literary work is made up of numerous books, transcripts and approximately 6000 lectures which have for the most part been edited and published in the Complete Works Edition.

Steiner's basic books, which were previously a prerequisite to gaining access to his lectures, are: *Theosophy, The Philosophy of Freedom, How to Know Higher Worlds, Christianity as a Mystical Fact,* and *Occult Science*.

ABOUT THE AUTHOR, DR. DOUGLAS GABRIEL

Dr. Gabriel is a retired superintendent of schools and professor of education who has worked with schools and organizations throughout the world. He has authored many books ranging from teacher training manuals to philosophical/spiritual works on the nature of the divine feminine.

He was a Waldorf class teacher and administrator at the Detroit Waldorf School and taught courses at Mercy College, the University of Detroit, and Wayne State University for decades. He then became the Headmaster of a Waldorf School in Hawaii and taught at the University of Hawaii, Hilo. He was a leader in the development of charter schools in Michigan and helped found the first Waldorf School in the Detroit Public School system and the first charter Waldorf School in Michigan.

Gabriel received his first degree in religious formation at the same time as an associate degree in computer science in 1972. This odd mixture of technology and religion continued throughout his life. He was drafted into and served in the Army Security Agency (NSA) where he was a cryptologist and systems analyst in signal intelligence, earning him a degree in signal broadcasting. After military service, he entered the Catholic Church again as a Trappist monk and later as a Jesuit priest where he earned PhD's in philosophy and comparative religion, and a Doctor of Divinity. As a Jesuit priest, he came to Detroit and earned a BA in anthroposophical studies and history and a MA in school administration. Gabriel left the priesthood and became a Waldorf class teacher and administrator in Detroit and later in Hilo, Hawaii.

Douglas has been a sought-after lecturer and consultant to schools and businesses throughout the world and in 1982 he founded the Waldorf Educational Foundation that provides funding for the publication of educational books. He has raised a great deal of money for Waldorf schools and institutions that continue to develop the teachings of Dr. Rudolf Steiner. Douglas is now retired but continues to write a variety of books including a novel and a science fiction thriller. He has four children, who keep him busy and active and a wife who is always striving towards the spirit through creating an "art of life." She is the author of the Gospel of Sophia trilogy.

The Gabriels' articles, blogs, and videos can currently be found at:

OurSpirit.com,
Neoanthroposphy.com,
GospelofSophia.com,
EternalCurriculum.com

TRANSLATOR'S NOTE

The Rudolf Steiner quotes in this book can be found, in most cases, in their full-length and in context, through the Rudolf Steiner Archives by an Internet search of the references provided. We present the quoted selections of Steiner from a free rendered translation of the original while utilizing comparisons of numerous German to English translations that are available from a variety of publishers and other sources. In some cases, the quoted selections may be condensed and partially summarized using the same, or similar in meaning, words found in the original. Brackets are used to insert [from the author] clarifying details or anthroposophical nomenclature and spiritual scientific terms.

We chose to use GA (Gesamtausgabe – collected edition) numbers to reference Steiner's works instead of CW (Collected Works), which is often used in English editions. Some books in the series, *From the Works of Rudolf Steiner*, have consciously chosen to use a predominance of Steiner quotes to drive the presentation of the themes rather than personal remarks and commentary.

We feel that Steiner's descriptions should not be truncated but need to be translated into an easily read format for the English-speaking reader, especially for those new to Anthroposophy. We recommend that serious aspirants read the entire lecture, or chapter, from which the Steiner quotation was taken, because nothing can replace Steiner's original words or the mood in which they were delivered. The style of speaking and writing has changed dramatically over the last century and needs updating in style and presentation to translate into a useful tool for spiritual study in modern times. The series, *From the Works of Rudolf Steiner* intends to present numerous "study guides" for the beginning aspirant, and the initiate, in a format that helps support the tool for spiritual study in modern times. The series, *From the Works of Rudolf Steiner* intends to present numerous "study guides" for the beginning aspirant, and the initiate, in a format that helps support the spiritual scientific research of the reader.

Made in the USA
Monee, IL
12 April 2024